Ghosts, Spirits and Hauntings

PATRICIA TELESCO

THE CROSSING PRESS
FREEDOM, CALIFORNIA

Copyright © 1999 Patricia Telesco
Cover illustration "Flying Dream" by Lena Bartula
Cover and interior design by Courtnay Perry
Printed in the USA

For information on bulk purchases or group discounts for this and other Crossing Press titles, please contact our Special Sales Manager at 800/777-1048.

Visit our website on the Internet: **www.crossingpress.com**

Library of Congress Cataloging-in-Publication Data

Telesco, Patricia, 1960-
    Ghosts, spirits, and hauntings / by Patricia Telesco.
        p. cm.
    Includes bibliographical references and index.
    ISBN 0-89594-871-0 (pbk.)
    1. Ghosts. 2. Spirits. I. Title
BF1461.T387   1999
133.1--dc21   99-33916
                                        CIP

Dedicated to the Spirit that motivates and inspires me,
with gratitude for the adventure that is
always beginning.

With special thanks to Fay, Dorothy, Judith, Colleen, Paul, and many others for their diligent efforts to find research materials or provide personal stories that illustrate the ideas in this book.

Contents

Out of the dusk a shadow,
    Then a spark;
Out of the clouds a silence,
    Then a lark;
Out of the heart a rapture,
    Then a pain;
Out of the dead, cold ashes,
    Life again.

—John Banister Tabb

Introduction

"The Soul is a bud of eternity."

—N. Culverwell

Belief in an afterlife permeates human history, and has shaped whole civilizations and religious systems. The world's greatest philosophers taught that the human spirit lives on after the body expires, and that another world waits for it beyond this life. As early as four thousand years ago, a Babylonian epic told the story of the hero Gilgamesh and his encounter with the spirit of a dead friend. Egyptians wrote instructions on papyrus, detailing how to appease an offending spirit by placing a note in its tomb. The lares and lemures, good and evil spirits, were familiar to Greek and Roman priests and magicians. In these, and many other cultures, dealing with the dead was an everyday skill, studied and practiced by the living.

This book is about the spirits who remain *between* this life and the afterlife, between the physical and etheric planes, between sound and silence. Such beings bear numerous names: ghosts, specters, phantoms, shades, spooks, or wraiths. By any name, this book acts as a guide to help you identify and cope with various types of ghosts, and to distinguish them from other spirits and phenomena.

Why do spirits linger in this world, rather than cross into the afterlife? Perhaps they don't know that they're dead. Perhaps they fear a new existence, or get inadvertently trapped on earth. Then, too, perhaps they may remain on earth deliberately, to finish some business, protect a person, guard an object, or stay close to a beloved place. Firsthand accounts of many such ghosts are included in this book. These were written by people who managed to understand their ghostly guest and resolve its issues favorably. I hope their stories encourage you to do the same.

Ghosts manifest differently, just as people communicate differently: some speak and some are silent; some roam and some are fettered to a place or object; some are visible and some remain unseen. Before you try dealing with a ghost it helps to know exactly what you are dealing with. There are some non-ghostly spirits, some false faces, that can easily be mistaken for ghosts. There are also environments that bear psychic imprints, a residual memory, often appearing ghostly in nature. The goal of this book is to help you distinguish a true haunting from these ghostly imposters.

Since most people develop a belief in ghosts only after having an encounter with one, I don't expect this book will turn non-believers into believers. James Martineau, an eighteenth century Unitarian minister, aptly said: "We do not believe in immortality because we have proved it, but we forever try to prove it because we believe it." A belief in ghosts is based on faith—our trust in the immutable nature of the human soul. Faith alone cannot verify or disprove the existence of ghosts or an afterlife; doubt alone cannot silence our lingering questions and our sense of wonder about what, if anything, happens to the human soul after death.

With this in mind, Chapters 2 and 3 of this book include a section called the Skeptical Advisor. This encourages you to consider possible natural, emotional, and environmental causes for an event you are dealing with; it is also a gentle reminder that, as you develop your sensitivity and understanding of hauntings, it helps to use common sense as a helpmate.

Whoever you are, and whatever your beliefs on this subject, I hope this book helps you become more familiar with the world of ghosts, spirits, and hauntings. If you are experiencing ghostly phenomena presently, these pages will help you understand what's going on and what action (if any) to take. If you wish to contact ghosts to impart messages or gain insights, there's assistance here for you too. Finally, even if you're just curious about ghosts and hauntings, this book is a mine that you can dig through, filled with the spiritual diamonds of folklore, traditions, and history.

So, pick up this book in moments when the unseen world touches the here and now, moments when the veil between worlds grows thin and trembles. Stand at those magical crossroads, listen to the voices of those who have passed over; listen to their stories. Listen when they ask us to see, act, and remember. Whatever you encounter, relate to it sensitively and intelligently, using this book as a guide. Then you will know what to do—how to disprove the phenomenon, live peacefully with a ghost, expel a spirit, or help a lost soul on toward the next reality.

CHAPTER I

The Elusive Soul

"Whatsoever that be within us that feels, thinks, desires and animates is something celestial and divine and consequently imperishable."

—Aristotle

"Life is the soul's nursery—its training place for the destinies of eternity."

—William Makepeace Thackeray

Your interest in ghosts has probably led you to question how the soul or spirit can survive the death of the body. You may be curious, too, about the nature of existence after death—or you may already have firm beliefs about this subject. Many of us are comforted by a belief that more waits for us after this life: we trust that our consciousness can survive death, or be independent of our limited mortal body.

The human soul—by that I mean the spark of life and individuality we all carry—may be capable of existing outside the human body. In many cultures, life after death is either an article of faith, or a working hypothesis. We have other traditions that argue the contrary: scientists have sifted the evidence for life after death and found nothing solid; psychologists have asserted that consciousness is just a by-product of the physical body.

Human knowledge has made great advances, but it still has no final answer to the questions posed by death. Can all that we have learned in our lifetime, all that we have become, simply fade away into nothingness? Although death is the natural outcome of our lives, we tend to dread it: or at least we wonder what, if anything, happens after death. When our bodies die, does our life come to a permanent end?

This chapter attempts to help you resolve those questions for yourself, by examining historical and cultural outlooks on the soul or spirit. I *do* accept the existence of ghosts, and write unashamedly from the standpoint of an ardent believer. But, in this survey of traditional beliefs about the nature of the spirit and the soul, I do not draw conclusions about their accuracy or value. I leave that for you to decide, for this is a matter of your own faith.

A Persistent Belief in the Soul

The earliest cultures we know of assumed that the dead had practical needs, and material and emotional requirements, in their new existence. For example, nearly 12,000 years ago, Stone Age communities buried their dead in fetal positions. Cro-Magnon people placed food and weapons with their dead. Funeral rites and burial observances expressed their faith in an afterlife, and in the ability of a departed spirit to return to this world. Death was just a temporary condition of separation from the world of the living.

When societies invented writing, they were able to record their beliefs in the continued existence of the soul. In 1500 B.C. the Vedas—religious writings of the Aryan migrants to India—explained that the individual soul (*atman*) must reincarnate until it reunites with the Divine (*Brahman*). Similarly Egyptians had an elaborate system of ritual for training and protecting the soul that had left the body. The Egyptian *Book of the Dead* is a guidebook for the soul's journey to the afterlife. Egyptian paintings from 1250 B.C. depict the *ba*—the astral body—as a bird hovering over the physical body after death.

The Etruscans, civilizers of Italy before the arrival of the Latins, had a highly developed priesthood, language, and set of ritual observances to deal with various sorts of spirits. These people painted the human spirit as an arch of light emanating from a living body. About 2,500 years later, Kirlian photography, which was developed in 1939, captured pictures of the human body surrounded by an aura of light. In the centuries between, artists from many cultures painted the spirit as a light radiating from the physical body. Paintings of the Buddha, of Indian and Tibetan yogis, and of Christian saints or desert hermits typically show them glorified by a halo. Around the seat of the divine at the crown of the head the human spirit takes on its true form—the radiant energy of light.

Note that in this book and many other studies, the words "soul" and "spirit" are often used interchangeably, perhaps because they both refer to non-physical states of being. Their usage has a confusing history, but it may help to distinguish the root meanings of the two words. The English word "spirit" comes from the Latin *spiritus*—meaning breath, disposition, and immaterial intelligence. It suggests a subtle, vital principle, not necessarily bound to our physical body, but alive and active. *Webster's Dictionary* defines "soul" as the center of will, the moral nature (that is, disposition), personality, emotions, and thought. "Soul" refers to the core of our individuality. So long as we are aware of ourselves as living, vital individuals, the terms "soul" and "spirit" cannot be kept rigidly separate: both words refer back to that basic awareness of our nature.

Most cultures see the soul as an entity that can separate from the physical body. Most agree, too, that the soul resembles the person who lived on earth—in its character, traits, and sometimes even in its appearance. There is a sort of dual nature to the soul—it can leave this world, but it has close ties to it. Some cultures say that, when the body dies, the soul moves on to a cosmic home—one of the cardinal directions, or a star or planet. Fox Indians, for example, believe that each person has two souls, one of which goes to the West after death. The Penobscot of New England feel that the soul abides as a star, apart from the mortal body.

Other native traditions emphasize the second quality of soul or spirit—its affinity to the physical body, and to the world of appearance. Breath is subtle and invisible, but without breath, we would not be alive. Spirit, like breath, is subtle, often invisible: it comes and goes from our body, and yet our body cannot live without it. Indians of the Mojave speak of the *shu'nun*, a soul that leaves the body with the last breath. Like the fetches of Scotland and England, the doppelgangers of German legend, or the spirits painted by the English author and visionary William Blake, the *shu'nun* exactly resembles the body of a living person.

But the Mojave also emphasize the soul's freedom from the body. They say that the soul escapes physical limitations during sleep, and that dreams and visions reflect the soul's nightly adventures. Cultures as widely separate as Australia, Siberia, and South America believe that the soul can leave the body and act independently of it. Once the soul has left, the mortal body is seen for what it is—a temporary residence for the individual. We often understand this when we are in the presence of someone who is dying.

A Safe Journey *The day before my father passed over, it became obvious that the end was near. He knew it; I knew it: neither of us could find words to fill the silent waiting. Just before I left that night, I wished him a good journey and godspeed.*

18

When I returned to the hospital to gather his personal belongings, I was struck by the appearance of the corpse in the bed. Try as I might, I could find nothing that remotely resembled my father. Yes, it was his face, his hair, his skin, but now it was just an empty shell—a form that no longer had visible substance. Dad truly was not in that dead flesh. I will forever remember that moment, especially in the years ahead when I face my own mortality. Now I know that the spirit moves on—where, I cannot be sure, but I don't need to know. The assurance is enough.

Images of the Hereafter

In 1990, nine percent of Americans surveyed said they had *seen* a ghost; more than twelve percent reported an experience of haunting. Among those millions of believers, there are certainly a wide variety of factors at work. Psychological studies indicate that people who are disturbed by the topic of death are more likely to believe in the paranormal and in existence after death. We may also believe in the afterlife because we have accepted the religious or cultural convictions that prevail among those around us. But many people, who are not in principle afraid of death, and who are relying only on the authority of their own experience, admit to unaccountable experiences that point to the soul's immortality. Reports come from all walks of life and regions of the globe: there is a widespread belief in the human spirit's ability to survive outside of the body, or after death.

When I was growing up, I believed that a beam of light breaking through the clouds meant that a soul was going to heaven. I don't know where I got this

Through the Clouds to God

idea—my parents were not ardent churchgoers. Nonetheless, from an early age I accepted the idea that I was more than mere flesh and blood, and that upon death something better would certainly await me.

I am about to give you a brief survey of religious and philosophical traditions about the afterlife: when you read these, I hope you remember that a child's images of the hereafter also deserve our respect.

Final Resting Places

Some religions present the hereafter as a fixed, permanent condition—a place where souls that have left this world remain forever. Many Christians believe in an eternal heaven and an eternal hell. Some Christians believe that there is a temporary purgatory, where sins are literally purged from the soul, so that it can ascend in a purified condition to an eternal heaven.

In Buddhist traditions, *nirvana* is a final condition of liberation: suffering is ended forever, and its causes are extinguished. For many schools of Buddhism, "*nirvana* is peace" is one of the defining tenets of their religion.

In China, Taoists believed in an Eden-like utopia, whose buildings were made of perfect jade—a sacred stone whose essence is pure love. Those who have achieved perfection can dwell here forever, eating the peaches of immortality.

Teutonic cultures believed that Valhalla was a final destination for brave souls. Warriors were brought there by the Valkyries—supernatural women in military dress, who appeared on the battlefield to take away the valiant warriors. The Valkyries were a kind of angelic guide, transporting the souls of dead heroes to a place where the supreme god Odin welcomed them with a drinking horn filled with mead.

Only distinguished warriors went to Valhalla; all other souls were consigned to *hel*—not a place of suffering or torture, but simply a residence for the spirits of the dead. The spirits in *hel* were able to interact with the living: some Germanic peoples even buried their dead under their threshold, so that the spirit would protect the house from harm. These spirits could appear in human or animal form.

Heavens and Hells

Most cultures did not think of heaven or hell as eternal destinations for the soul. These were places of reward and punishment for past actions: after a limited period of suffering or of enjoyment, the spirit moved on to another existence. The Upanishads—philosophical writings founded on the Vedic hymns—described heavens where the soul enjoyed rewards for its past actions. After a period of bliss, which could be enormously long, the soul was reborn elsewhere, to continue the cycle of reincarnation. Heaven, while pleasant, was not final: the desired goal was perfect union with *Brahman.*

Vedic philosophers believed that there were many heavens and many hells, and that none of these were eternal. This view, adopted by the Hindus and Buddhists of later India, spread to the Buddhists of Japan, China, and Tibet. In Japan, devotees pray to be reborn in the Western Paradise of Amitabha Buddha—a Pure Land where it is easy to attain liberation.

Saviors and savioresses make regular visits to the Chinese, Japanese, and Tibetan hells, to rescue spirits consigned there. Chinese believe that Ti'tsang, a compassionate god, goes in search of souls that have strayed into one of the hells, and rescues them from suffering.

From Asia, the notion that there were many heavens and many hells, specifically suited to a being's past actions, migrated west. It was found among Zoroastrians in Iran, and in some schools of Islamic thought. It eventually found its way into Italy, and was adopted, in *The Divine Comedy*, by the Christian poet Dante Alghieri.

Reincarnation

Hindus, Jains, Buddhists, Druids, Pythagoreans, Celts, Gnostics, Jewish Cabalists, Spiritualists, and some early Christian sects have all believed that death is followed by rebirth. After death, individuals retain all their memories and knowledge in some part of their makeup. Upon rebirth, these memories and habits are subconscious, but still influence the pattern of life. People can fix their mistakes from previous existences, and emphasize their positive tendencies: in many ways, this is the ultimate in effective recycling.

Most people, however, don't readily remember specifics from their past lives: they write off the partial memories that sneak into consciousness as odd dreams or déjà vu. A Chinese tradition holds that, during the interval between one incarnation and the next, a spirit drinks from the cup of oblivion that erases memories of the previous life. This loss of memory makes the soul's quest for reunion with the Divine difficult.

Spirits of the dead, in Chinese lore, look for new bodies to incarnate in—sometimes among the living. There is a tradition that, after three years in the underworld, a ghost may return to the place of its death, in order to find another spirit to take its place. This is why it became customary, in China, to avoid regions where murders and violent crimes were committed—these were considered heavily haunted and quite dangerous to the living.

Most cultures that believe in reincarnation think that, between lives, the soul spends time in an intermediate state. Cultures differ as to where it goes, or how long it spends there—weeks, or centuries. Hindus believe that cremation temporarily releases the spirit to the sun or stars, where it remains until it takes on a new body. Not all cultures agree that the spirit and the living can communicate during this transitional period.

In Africa, the people of the Murdahg tribe believe that the souls of the dead go into a hole. Here souls wait until they can enter a female body and create new life. While it waits, the soul is not believed to be capable of communicating with the living. Animal as well as human souls go through this process, although animals may only take an animal body; humans must select a human body.

Polynesian cultures speak of the soul's transition after death as a long journey, part of which takes place on earth, and part in the next world. In the earthly part of its journey, the spirit has a chance of being reborn a mortal, usually by making some moral or symbolic choice. Like Persephone of Greek mythology, the Polynesian soul must decide whether to eat a certain fruit, which will determine the course of its afterlife. The fruit is one of a number of tests the soul undergoes during this transitional period. The Polynesians, like the Murdahg, do not seem to believe that souls in an intermediate state can communicate with the world of the living.

The belief in reincarnation is not limited to tribal and Asian cultures. In Western civilization, it has attracted a variety of believers including Alfred Lord Tennyson, William Butler Yeats, Thomas Edison, and George Patton. Patton specifically believed that a past incarnation as a Roman legionnaire contributed to his success as an American general. These men subscribed to the essential belief of all the ancient traditions of reincarnation—that the past life influences the present, just as this present life will influence the future.

Guillianna's Fear

For as long as I can remember, my best friend has been afraid of heights. One day we were talking about past lives and tried a brief meditation to see if we could understand the source of Guillianna's fear, as nothing had happened in real time to induce it. As we worked through the visualization, Guillianna found herself in the body of a young girl looking at a tall ladder leading into a loft. Another child ran up behind her. As Guillianna climbed the ladder, the other child pulled accidentally on her shoe, causing her to fall and break her neck. She died instantly.

The results of this meditation were astounding to us, as Guillianna had never told me she was also afraid of being approached from behind, and of falling. While the meditation did not erase the fears, it did provide her with a helpful frame of understanding, which enabled her to deal with the fears more effectively.

The Spirit Outside the Body During Life

"When we live, we sleep; when we die, we wake."

—Mohammed

NDEs (NEAR-DEATH EXPERIENCES) If we perceive or communicate with the spirit of someone who has died, but is still waiting to take on a new body, that is a "ghostly" phenomenon. If, during life, the spirit leaves the body, then it belongs to the class of "non-ghostly" spirits. We will meet a host of these in "The Spectral Register," the second chapter of this book.

Non-ghostly spirits can be produced by two fascinating phenomena—Near-Death Experiences (NDEs) and Out-of-Body Experiences (OBEs). These experiences suggest that the soul can leave, and later return to, the body. If we encountered a spirit detached from the body by an OBE or NDE, it would be a "non-ghostly" visitor.

Writings about near-death experiences are as old as writings about the afterlife. Ancient guidebooks on the art of dying include descriptions of what happens to the spirit in the moments near death. This is a special transitional state, in which the spirit leaves the body, but may not yet realize what is happening. From this special vantage point, the spirit can often see over the horizon of the afterlife, and into the next world. In Egypt, the *Book of the Dead* described what the spirit experiences before it begins its journeys and trials in the afterlife. Plato's *Republic* gives the account of a man named Er, who was dead for twelve days. He was placed on a funeral pyre, where he revived suddenly and told the gathered crowd how he left his body and saw the afterlife. During the sixth century A.D.,

Pope Gregory the Great collected reports of unusual experiences, three of which were NDEs.

There is a revival of interest in NDEs in the twentieth century. American novelist Ernest Hemingway described coming near death during World War I: during this experience, he left his body. During the 1970s, Raymond Moody, the author of *Life After Life*, made systematic studies of NDEs, and drew public attention to the phenomenon. Moody found these experiences to resemble each other closely, despite wide variations in the cultural backgrounds of the people who experienced them. People who undergo NDEs typically sense a buzzing or vibration, as a preliminary sensation. Next, they see their own body, from which they are now freed. Now disembodied, the spirit may encounter other entities, often from his or her family. Afterwards there is typically a passage through darkness or a tunnel, and into the radiance of a vibrant light, or an indescribable presence. A feeling of peace or joy comes at this moment, sometimes accompanied by panoramic visions of the individual's life.

The typical progression that Moody found in NDEs parallels much of the so-called "Tibetan Book of the Dead." Tibetans read this book to a dying person, and for forty-nine days after death, to guide them toward liberation and to keep them from becoming confused by the apparitions that arise. The book discusses how to deal with many of the issues Moody chronicled—shock or surprise, loss of the physical body, and emotional attachment to relatives. The dying person is encouraged to recognize the basic luminosity that dawns immediately after death, and to attain liberation from rebirth.

OBEs (Out-of-Body Experiences) Out-of-Body Experiences, also called astral projections, suggest that the spirit can exist outside the body. To exist after death, the spirit has to be able to leave, and remain viable outside of, the body. The body is discovered to be but a temporary anchor for the inner self, which can voyage apart from it.

Some Biblical passages support this theory. The prophet Ezekiel reported that God carried him by the hair to Jerusalem. The apostle Paul rose up to the third heaven: he wrote that he did not know whether this journey took place in or out of his body. Gnostics developed meditative practices to release the spirit from the trap of matter. The Christian church sometimes took a dim view of these excursions: during the Middle Ages, monks were chastised for leaving their bodies to view heaven and hell. Such explorations of divine mysteries were associated with the sin of curiosity.

Among the class of paranormal experiences they called *riddhi*, Buddhists include OBEs. During this experience, a person may pass through solid objects, walk on water, and fly.

In the late 1800s, the Theosophical Society experimented with a form of astral projection in which the spirit moved out from the body, attached to a silver cord. If this cord was severed, death ensued. In recent years, OBE research began to move away from occult language and theory, and to adopt scientific paradigms. The status of such research as serious science is disputed, because the evidence for OBEs consists mainly of reports of subjective experience. Still, the great number of similar reports—which come from many times and many civilizations—encourages serious researchers to adopt the hypothesis that "the soul is able to leave the body."

OBEs have several distinctive features. In a typical onset, a person feels fuzzy or tingly and hears odd clicking sounds. Next, the consciousness seems to be instantaneously—sometimes abruptly—removed from the body. In nearly all cases, the person remains completely relaxed: his mind is not preoccupied with bodily sensations throughout the OBE, and is freed to attend to the imagery of the experience. The self and consciousness become an energy-centered reality instead of a physically-centered reality.

People tend to find themselves in a familiar location—such as their bedroom—at the beginning of an OBE. Typically, they quickly discover an ability to travel great distances with but a thought. The end of the OBE is sometimes reported to have been abrupt: something brought the spirit back to the body suddenly. Many OBEs are unexpected and unsought events; some people, however, have mastered the technique of leaving and entering the body at will.

Just a Dream?

I remember "dreaming" once that I was flying far more quickly than my eyes could comprehend. I was moving, trying to find the sobbing voice of a young girl in distress. Once I found the voice, I knew the surroundings were strange and that I wasn't wholly physical. Yet that girl seemed to be aware of a "presence"—which she may have later considered some type of ghost.

After our encounter, I found myself flying again, and then felt a hard snap—as though a rubber band had been pulled too tightly. At this point I sat straight up in bed with a terrible headache. When I awoke completely, the experience remained with me as clearly as if I'd walked to the girl. Perhaps she was a ghost...perhaps I was a spirit or angel to her...in either case, that moment changed my outlook on the limits we place on human consciousness.

Further Inquiry

While none of the religious or social views presented in this chapter offer conclusive proof of the existence of ghosts and spirits, they do give us some good reasons to reconsider our ideas about human mortality and the afterlife. I offer the following points for contemplation:

Reincarnation

(The idea that we have lived before is supported by reports of former existences from very young children, who might say, "when I was an old woman..." or "when you and I were sisters...."

(The last incident of an incarnation—the moment it ended—is usually retrieved at the beginning of a past-life recall. Recent memories are easier to retrieve than more distant memories: if we have lived— and died—before, the deathbed scene would be the most recent.

(The theory of reincarnation, which holds that past lives influence our present circumstances, reminds us that we shape our own destinies. If misfortunes occur, we don't attribute them to cruel fate or inscrutable forces.

(Conservation of energy is one of the laws of the physical universe. Energy cannot be created or destroyed: it simply changes form. Into what form does the human consciousness change?

OBEs

(The astral body, during an OBE, is transmitted through a different dimension. It is just as real, and just as elusive, as a radio signal in the atmosphere: if we have no receiver, we do not detect it, even though it exists.

(OBEs are similar to NDEs in many ways, but their cause is different. This could indicate that separation of the spirit from the physical body is a real phenomenon with definite characteristics.

(Astral travelers reported the sensation of flying, long before the invention of mechanical flight. Their subjective descriptions resemble closely the experience of flying in a modern machine. How did they know what it was like to fly?

NDEs

(People who experience NDEs are more likely to begin experiencing paranormal abilities like precognition or telepathy afterwards. What is it about the NDE that encourages spiritual awakening?

(Young children, most of whom have no cultural expectations or preconceived notions of what an NDE should entail, also experience the typical NDE pattern.

(Some people who have NDEs do not recognize their own bodies right away. Yet we recognize our bodies immediately, if we see them in a mirror. It *is* difficult to recognize the body, when it is seen from an unfamiliar perspective. This could suggest that NDEs afford a special, external perspective on the body.

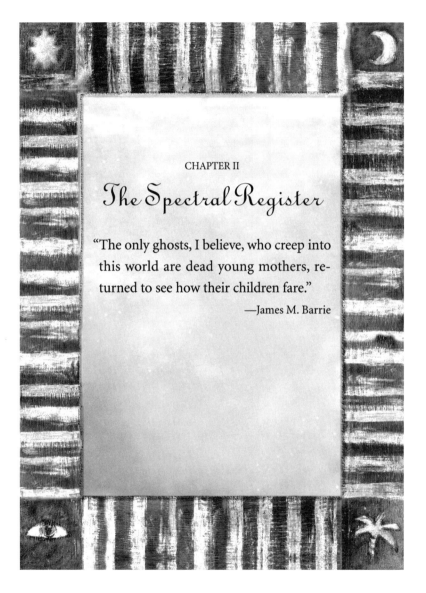

CHAPTER II

The Spectral Register

"The only ghosts, I believe, who creep into this world are dead young mothers, returned to see how their children fare."

—James M. Barrie

It seems that not all souls go "gentle into that good night," as the living might hope. Ghosts are as complicated as mortals, and return to this world for a wide variety of reasons. Untimely or violent deaths leave behind a traumatized or bewildered spirit. Ghosts worried about their kin stay close by—watching, protecting, and guiding those they love. A spirit that didn't complete its life's work might linger in the hope of encouraging someone else to finish or perfect the task.

This chapter examines these and other types of ghosts in depth. I have included personal accounts, to provide you with a frame of reference and with specific examples. When you compare your own encounters with ghosts to the entries in this chapter, please remember that your encounter with a ghost—or ghosts—will probably resemble one or more of the types I have given. What you experience will also have unique traits. The personality of the ghost, the situation you encounter it in, and your own interpretive perspective on the incident—these combine to give your experience its distinctive character.

I have placed a small section called "Skeptical Advisor" after my description of each type of ghost. This section is not meant, in any way, to undermine the sincerity of the personal accounts, or the power of those experiences. I offer these alternative explanations so you can develop your psychological insight. Once you have a stable foundation—a mix of belief and rationality—for your investigations, you can establish a method for tracking down and resolving the mysteries presented by hauntings.

Angry Ghosts

These spirits linger in this world, displaying their anger like a badge of honor. The anger has various causes, and takes various forms—indignation toward family members who bickered around the deathbed about the will, fury toward someone who harmed them emotionally or physically, or simply rage at the fact that they are dead. Sometimes a ghost's anger is not directed toward the living: one psychic tells of a woman whose spirit refused to cross over, because her cheating husband would be waiting for her on the other side! Her pride and resentment led her to choose limbo.

For angry ghosts to move on, it is imperative that they forgive others, or liberate themselves from the bitterness that binds them. For ghosts, this is not a simple task. Ghosts, by their very nature, are even more prone to habit, and stuck in their ways, than mortals. Reasoning them out of their grudge may be difficult: these spirits want recompense for their pain and, like all ghosts, have very long memories.

A séance may help an angry ghost. The medium can call on living family members to make amends, if necessary. The medium might contact spirits of the dead, and reconcile them with the angry ghost. Finally, the medium can try to talk directly to this spirit and learn more of its "story." Very often angry ghosts have a tale to tell, and may just want *someone* to hear it for once. Angry ghosts release negative energy when they can recount their tale: it is something like taking a knot out of a balloon. The emotional deliverance may be enough to allow the angry ghost to move on.

Skeptical Advisor: Anger is a natural human emotion. If the spirit you encounter seems upset about something that also upsets you, then the manifestation may be caused by your own subconscious, expressing itself through a "safer" medium.

Concerned Ghosts

The concerned ghost is likely one who fretted about everyone and everything in life—the proverbial "mother-hen" type. This spirit truly believes that the living cannot possibly get on successfully without its help. The concerned ghost may not have resolved its relationship with the person it pays such fastidious attention to. These ghosts are fettered to this world by the proverbial apron strings.

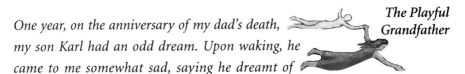

The Playful Grandfather

One year, on the anniversary of my dad's death, my son Karl had an odd dream. Upon waking, he came to me somewhat sad, saying he dreamt of grandpa and missed him. When asked what the dream was about, Karl reported that his grandfather indicated liking Karl very much, and hoped they could be playmates.

This was very significant to me. When Karl was a baby, my dad— who had rheumatoid arthritis—could never play with him or hold him. Dad was cranky because he was so sick. Now, in Karl's dream time, dad was able to fulfill the role of grandfather as he wished to in life. Karl finally got to see what his grandfather was really like. To this day, Karl's dream-time encounters with grandpa are the ones he remembers; he does not remember the sickly, cantankerous old man.

To break a concerned ghost's spiritual apron strings, convince it beyond all doubt that all will be well in its absence. When there are unresolved personal issues, the spirit has to find a way to meet the need it perceives—as my father did, in the story above. In the next account, Fay Esan tells how her mother fulfilled a promise to her.

Knock Three Times

My mother suffered congestive heart failure when she was 61, and had a heart attack six months later. Upon returning home from the hospital, we began to speculate about what lies ahead when we die. She laughed, saying that, if she passed on before I did, she would let me know that there was an afterlife—by knocking three times. This signal would tell me she was with me, and all was well. Of course I agreed to do the same, should I go first.

In September of 1975, mom called me downstairs wanting to talk about a vision she had the night before. She was in a long dark corridor, with people before and behind her. Ahead was a door that, when opened, revealed the most beautiful garden imaginable, filled with flowers, trees, brooks, and happy people. As she attempted to cross the threshold of the doorway, a figure stopped her and said it was not yet time, but would be soon. The figure gently pulled her out of line and sent her back. At this point mom found herself in bed, taking the vision as a portent of her death. Not long thereafter she had another heart attack and was pronounced dead at the hospital.

Six months later, I was suddenly wakened from my sleep. When I looked around, a shadowy figure appeared at my bedside. As soon as my eyes focused on the figure, I heard three resounding raps on the nightstand. That was mom's signal, letting me know that consciousness did, indeed, go on after death. Her promise was fulfilled.

—Fay Esan

Skeptical Advisor: We all would enjoy knowing that a guardian angel stood by to comfort or protect us in times of need. The ghost of a well-loved family member would be a reassuring presence. The early memories of children—such as my son Karl—are far more precise and long-lived than we previously imagined. Karl could have gotten, in a dream, what he wished his grandfather had done with him in life. Fay may have dreamt the three knocks, prompted by a subconscious need for assurance.

Evolved Ghosts

The evolved ghost is a unique spirit: it is not trapped here, but stays of its own choice. During life, the evolved ghost reached a peak spiritual state. It could return to oneness with the Source, but it has postponed that reunion, for noble reasons.

The Hopi Shaman

I was fortunate and blessed in earlier years to spend time in Arizona studying with a shaman. At the end of my stay on the reservation, the shaman died and was laid to rest on a pyre, with his feathered cloak and walking stick. I felt an emptiness inside; this man had been a mentor and father figure for nearly a year.

Later that evening I went out into the desert and gazed at the ceiling of stars. As I stood there, a nearly solid image of grandfather appeared on the sands and smiled at me. He said nothing, but wrapped his cloak around himself and transformed into a huge black raven, his totem bird. Then he flew into the heavens.

Somehow I knew I would be seeing more of him. Sure enough, no matter where I lived a big black crow always showed up in a nearby tree, cawing incessantly at 6 A.M. Sometimes electrical items randomly went on and off to announce his presence.

When I married, it was difficult to convince my wife of the truth of my personal haunting...until the shaman appeared in our living room! I came home from work one night to find my wife sitting in a rocking chair, mumbling about a smiling, withered old man with feathered cloak and staff, who politely disappeared when she begged the vision to go away. While she was visibly shaken by the experience, at least now both of us believed in our guardian spirit and prankster. Before this encounter I'm pretty sure my wife thought I was a little crazy!

The crow and the electrical problems followed us in our married life from one apartment to another, and even into our home. Lights and television sets switch on or off, seemingly of their own free will—especially those I had just turned off or on moments before! This is harmless humor from the shaman's spirit, who delights in reminding me of my humanity.

One bright summer day when our daughter was toddling by an open window, she heard grandpa's call. Samantha ran expectantly to that window, and tried to answer the crow's caw. This went on for several minutes. To this day I have no idea what grandfather was telling her, but I don't need to know. It seems his spirit is now watching over and teaching our children in the way of the shaman—truly a gift from beyond, for which I am grateful.

—Taka

Skeptical Advisor: These experiences could be explained as coincidences rearranged by Taka's hopeful, imaginative mind. Children regularly mimic animals, and there is no rule that says crows can't live wherever they wish! Still, Taka's wife was a skeptic who saw the shaman. This, and the fact that the experiences have recurred for 13 years, make the story hard to doubt.

Evolved ghosts may also reflect our Higher Self, not a spiritual entity.

Fearful Ghosts

Some ghosts hold on to this world because they fear the transition death brings. This seems especially common among ghosts who were the victims of sudden or untimely deaths. Ghosts who died in preventable accidents may worry that someone else will suffer their fate, and remain to watch and ward the area they died in.

When I was in college I lived in an apartment **Guardian of the Stairway** *where a plethora of odd occurrences took place. The disturbances were minor, and I knew little of ghosts at that time, so I tried to shrug the whole matter off.*

One day a guest asked me if the house was haunted. I wondered what inspired such an odd question. My guest told her story: she had seen a

39

white, transparent figure hovering near the kitchen door, which led to the back stairwell. The image appeared to be an older man.

I did not understand this incident, until one day the presence and reason for this ghost became undeniably clear. One afternoon I was taking my dirty clothing downstairs to the washing machine. Between the second and first floor landing, my foot missed a stair and I found myself falling. Just as I thought I would land flat on my nose, I felt a cold, solid barrier meet my leg, supporting it until I could get my footing.

I sat down immediately on the stairs, still shaking and trying to understand why this presence chose to protect me. As I pondered, images filled my mind of an elderly man falling down the same set of stairs to an immediate death. His spirit remained behind as the guardian of that stairway, always fearing that someone else would be injured on that spot.

From that day forward, I honored my ghostly protector in every way I could, even posting a sign on the back stairway for people to watch their step. I don't know if the spirit appreciated the gesture, but it certainly made me feel better. I often drive by that house even today, and can still sense his presence lingering nearby, standing watch.

Ghosts who are afraid of transition need to see that there is nothing to fear. It is not easy to convince them: try convincing a living person that death is but a doorway, with a new existence on the other side! Ghosts who hesitate at the threshold of the afterlife can be helped when a psychic opens a doorway into the realm of Light, and shows the spirit what awaits it.

Honoring the ghost's feelings—for instance, by putting warning signs on the stairway it is haunting—may also resolve the situation.

The protective, guardian ghost has other needs: it must feel confident that whatever caused its demise will not occur again. The haunted area may require architectural changes that ensure safety and solidity. A ghost may find rest after a traffic signal is installed at the intersection where it died. Once the danger is eliminated, the ghost has no reason to linger.

Skeptical Advisor: Most adults feel silly admitting they fear venturing into cold, dark basements; yet this is a very common feeling. We may project that fear, creating the thought-form of the protective, guardian variety of fearful ghost. Ghosts who merely fear the transition to the other world could be projections of our own apprehensions about the afterlife. We don't always know our own fears. It is possible that our subconscious tendencies, or trauma originating in our past lives, may be at the bottom of a haunting.

Fettered Ghosts

The fettered ghost attaches itself emotionally, through a line of energy, to a person, a place, or a thing. The Banshee is a fettered ghost. Scottish tradition has it that a Banshee binds itself to a family line, appearing and uttering its distinctive wail just prior to a family member's death. The Banshee is fettered to ancestry and to a specific task.

It is hardest to break fetters to people. You can change a place or object—physically or psychically—but a person might object strongly to your proposed renovation! He may be able to break the connection himself, if he tells the ghost repeatedly that it is not wanted. Rejection, as ruthless as it may seem, is a potent emotional tool to which ghosts are not immune. If a person is unable to break the link on his own, a psychic or medium can be called in to help.

If a ghost is fettered to a place, ask why this location is important to the ghost. Did it live, or die, there? Did it build all or part of that structure? Did a loved one live there for a long time? If the ghost is intimately connected to a place, it may be best to let it live there in peace, so long as it lets the living do the same.

"Freddy" the Founding Father?

In the late 1970s I lived in a small town just north of Houston, Texas. The house I rented was awful. It had dark, dingy colors, and was desperately in need of TLC. So I went immediately to work, armed with buckets of white paint. I can't tell you how many times brushes and rollers tipped out of my hands. Being somewhat clumsy I didn't think much of these problems and went right on working, covering the darkness of the previous tenants.

After a week, the house was finished. I kicked back, very pleased with the bright clean walls, curtains, and fresh air now coming through the windows. Thrilled with the results, I put on some coffee and treated myself to a long hot shower.

After emerging, I noticed a cup of steaming hot coffee on the counter. I hadn't poured it. Not only wasn't the coffee ready when I took my shower, but my coffee mugs weren't even unpacked yet! This threw me into a panic. I thought for certain someone had broken in—someone gutsy enough to help himself to coffee! I slipped through the house, towel-clad, looking like John Wayne on the hunt, but turned up nothing.

A few nights later I woke to find a very tall man at the foot of my bed. His curly red hair flipped out from under a double-brimmed cap—the type that Basil Rathbone wore in Sherlock Holmes movies. His long arms emerged from the rolled-up sleeves of his plaid flannel shirt. When I reached for my gun, he just smiled and disappeared.

This experience put me into research mode. I started delving into the town's history. Apparently a former sidekick of Red Adair—a famous firefighter—bought a parcel of land and built the town. He got an excellent deal on old logging cabins nearby and moved them onto the property. Whether this ghost was that man, or Red himself, I couldn't be certain. I took to calling him "Freddy."

Freddy showed up regularly, rarely causing trouble. However, I once had a male friend over, whom Freddy didn't like. Freddy rushed toward a swag lamp hanging over the man's head. I got my friend out of the chair just in time, and was furious with Freddy. In retrospect I should have paid attention to Freddy's opinion. The guy turned out to be a jerk.

After I moved, I never saw Freddy again. The house has burned down, and I wonder from time to time if Freddy is still there in its ruins. I hope not. Such a nice ghost deserves the peace and pleasure of final rest.

—Dorothy

This ghost was attached to a house that had been an intimate part of his life. He simply didn't have the heart to leave. "Freddy" found his version of paradise in his own back yard.

Fetters to objects are the easiest to handle. If the object is portable, return it to the ghost's grave, or to its living relative. If the object is too big to relocate—a statue or fountain, for instance—try using a picture of the item instead. Enclose the photograph in plastic covering to protect its longevity, then return it to the burial place or to a nearby location. This may keep the ghost from wandering. Plastic is not as earth friendly as I'd like, but it is important to preserve the photograph carefully so it lasts as long as possible.

Ghostly Animals, Objects, and Vehicles

Apparitions of animals, objects, and vehicles can be due to energy imprints: such projections, although we observe them, are not caused by an entity interacting with this world. The regular reappearance of the *Titanic* might come under this category.

A nearby spirit may, however, be fettered to a ghostly animal, object, or vehicle. Ghosts are especially likely to be fettered to pets, which are typically well-beloved companions. It is an open question whether the ghost is attached to the pet's spirit (if you believe animals have spirits) or to its energy imprint.

Dog Days

We began moving into our new home during the summer, and one of the first major projects was to replace the old overgrown wire fence. One day, while cleaning out the area around the gate, I saw a golden retriever out of the corner of my eye. I turned to see if the dog had tags—we get a lot of strays in the city—but he wasn't there. I shrugged, thinking the dog must have run off, and resumed my work. Again, I saw the dog to my left, panting happily, but taking no notice of me. I didn't understand this until later, when I saw pictures of previous residents of the house. Among the photographs, there was one picture of a beautiful golden retriever sitting happily in the old yard with his young master, in the same spot, holding the same stance, as when I saw him. While I couldn't call this a ghost, it was certainly an impression of a very contented pet left on the house and land.

Communal thought-forms can be created when objects and vehicles generate intense emotion in many people at once. These have more dimension than energy imprints, but they are not ghosts. The ghostly image of Lincoln's funeral train was created by the saturation of the region with human emotion. The object or animal may be part of a ghost's story. In life, a person might have carried a hand mirror moments before death, or might have been walking the family dog when a heart attack struck. So, if you see or sense specific items or animals, these may well have a spirit to whom they belong, and who uses these shadows to recount a personal tragedy.

Skeptical Advisor: We can forget that a beloved pet has died, and come home to find it happily wagging its tail in the window. That apparition disappears when we remember that the animal is dead. The image might be a vividly detailed memory, projected at a suitable time and place. This sort of memory is like the phenomenon of "phantom limbs." Nerves fire according to memory, creating the illusion that the missing body part is still attached. Our memories of a missing pet may trigger nerve-impulses, causing us to sense a "ghostly" imposter.

Malevolent Ghosts

Of all things that send chills up the spines of the living, images of demonic, disfigured, screeching spooks are high on the list. Many religions, believing that goodness only has meaning when balanced against evil, have filled their writings with the imagery of malevolent spirits. The Arabic word "*ghoul*" comes from a verb meaning "to seize": that is exactly what ghouls are reputed to do—they seize the bodies of unsuspecting victims. These fiends were prevalent in stories from Asia and the Middle East.

In medieval Europe, goblins and imps roamed freely, as did a type of demon known as the incubus—a predator somewhat similar to a vampire. The Scandinavian *utburd* is the sickly, vengeful ghost of a miscarried infant: its cries are piercing. The only defense against an *utburd* is to splash quickly into a stream and unsheathe an iron knife. The Slavic version of the *utburd* is a *navky*. A *navky* is the soul of an unbaptized child, or one murdered by his or her mother. It wails and cries in trees, sometimes taking the shape of a bird, sometimes begging travelers for aid.

In Icelandic tradition, "sendings" are evil spirits, created and given mobility by a necromancer. These are not ghosts, but magical creations used for revenge. The only way to eliminate this heinous spirit is to thrust iron into its central white spot—the heart of this unnatural being.

Today, we still hear tales of monsters under the bed, and demons in a fiery abyss. It is hard to understand why such malevolent creatures would wish to visit earth. Do they feed on fear, like some form of psychic vampire? Do they revel in human misery? What motivates a malevolent specter, or a vile-appearing spirit, to intervene in human affairs?

Five plausible answers exist. First, the spirit may represent a person disfigured in life—especially shortly before death. The deformed appearance may become a powerful image, which follows the spirit into the beyond like an astral energy imprint. If externals were very important to the spirit during life, these imprints are especially likely to occur after death.

Some people are just plain nasty by nature, during life. Such individuals form a second class of vile apparition. When such spirits are present, our conscious mind reacts to their offensive personality by forming an ugly image—darkness, or slimy coldness, for example. Very angry ghosts can develop very ugly faces as bitterness eats away at what little is left of their humanity.

A third consideration: a spirit's grotesque appearance may be just a byproduct of a natural process—the body's decay after death. The tattered clothes and flesh remind us of the frailness of our mortal form. It is as if the ghost is saying, "As I am, so you shall be." We may take this as a hostile message, and class the spirit as malevolent, if we feel threatened by reminders that our life is limited.

The fourth sort of hideous image is not a ghost, but a thought form created by a leakage of negative psychic energy. This malevolent spirit stays close to its creator, like a hovering black cloud. Once the energy source for the negativity is eliminated, the personal demon will fade.

Fifth and finally, a malevolent spirit may indeed represent the flip side of goodness—an astral being who tests the mettle of human mortality, and against whose dark powers we must battle, using drastic measures. Scandinavians would resort, in these cases, to an exorcism of a house or object, called an *at manened*. This term means, literally, "to force down": in this procedure, the spirit is returned to the earth.

Within a Breath's Moment

As a 14-year-old, I had a particularly frightening experience. At first I thought I was dreaming. In the room where I slept, a dark figure loomed nearby, terribly disfigured and hideous in appearance. I tried to speak or yell for help, but the weight of a hand stopped all my efforts—even though I could see no hand. The presence near my face was so strong I felt sure I would faint from lack of air. My fears led me at first to struggle, but then suddenly I realized that no unearthly power could silence my mind. So I "thought" to the spirit, and commanded it away using traditional Christian prayers and admonitions. For whatever reason, the spirit obeyed and abated. To this day I do not know what I encountered or why, but it never returned.

> *Skeptical Advisor:* From a purely psychological view, evil manifestations might be expressions of our own fears, "deadly sins," guilt, and inner ugliness whose face we prefer not to show to the world. Being unable to move or act effectively may also reflect subconscious issues stemming from being stifled, silenced, or not adequately expressing emotions or ideas.

Story Ghosts

The story ghost has a tale to tell. For any number of reasons, story ghosts feel that the events of their life, or those that took them into death, are important and need to be shared. Until someone hears and truly understands this ghost's account, the narrative remains a fetter tying their spirit to earth.

The Rocking Horse

My nephew David and his wife, Kelly, asked for my help in remedying a suspected haunted house. In response to her request, I contacted Trish (the author of this book) and her husband, Paul, for advice. They volunteered to come out and investigate the site for a small fee—some homemade cookies!

The house is located in Basom, New York. The family living there has two small children, both of whom talked of an invisible playmate, a young boy. There were repeated sightings of a man walking from the living room into the kitchen and disappearing through a wall, and numerous cold spots throughout the house with no apparent cause. Also, an old woman was seen gazing from the upstairs window into the back yard, and in the basement a woman wearing a long dress appeared. None of these spirits communicated; they just dissolved or periodically slammed doors.

Paul and Trish came to the house with Kelly, Dave, and my nephew Jimmy. As we approached the house, Paul saw an old man driving a horse and buggy at a gallop down the road; he drove at an ever faster pace, as if to beat us to the house. The specter glared as we passed, then faded from view.

A psychic inspection of the house and its cold spots revealed many startling things. The old woman upstairs was the grandmother of a family of former residents. She had a lovely garden in the back yard when she was alive, and she loved to look at it from her window. Placing fresh flowers in her room, or planting a few outside, would keep this spirit happy, as she had no intentions of leaving "her home."

The rest of the story was more complex. Apparently the father of this family served in the Civil War. While he was gone, he left his wife, and his young son Jonathan, in the care of his brother. The uncle tried desperately to be kind to the boy, even though he was not good with children. Meanwhile, the wife was secretly using the basement as a way-station for escaped slaves.

One day, the uncle came visiting with a lovely rocking horse for Jonathan, who quickly moved to the head of the stairs to see his gift. The little boy was so excited that he began running down the stairs and fell to his death. Shortly thereafter, the uncle discovered his sister-in-law's deception, and hanged one of the ex-slaves from a gnarled tree in back of the house. He blamed the war for everything, and his anger was driven by his grief over the boy's death.

As we discussed the situation, we noticed that almost all the pictures in the house depicted rocking horses and little black girls. There was even a child-sized rocking horse near the living-room hearth, as a decoration! We quickly moved the rocking horse into the kitchen, where Jonathan could play with it. Immediately thereafter a rush of cool air came down the staircase, accompanied by a nearly audible giggle. The rocking horse remains here, accompanied by pine incense—the boy's mother had bathed him in pine soap—to this day.

Out back, Trish and Paul instructed the family to dig up the hideous old tree, and the anger associated with it: they used it to fertilize a garden. Now beauty could grow where only prejudice and grief had been. Flowers were also taken upstairs to the grandmother's room, for her enjoyment.

As we left, a sense of peace fell over the house. The scent of pine—the aroma of Jonathan's mother—greeted us as we opened the front door. Jonathan finally got to thank his uncle for his toy, and the uncle could focus on that, instead of on the bitterness that had bound him to this world. Since then, the family has had no problems with visions, doors, or drafts. The ghost's story has been told, and everyone has been given rest.

—Fay

When the story ghost's tale is told, this breaks the repetitive energy imprints that are part of its fetter. The resulting effect on the environment is rather like taking the needle off a scratched, skipping record, as Fay and her nephew's family discovered. Story ghosts, once you unfetter them, either settle down contentedly, or move on.

Fay describes an interesting situation in which *all* the unfettered ghosts chose to stay right where they were. Jonathan stayed because his spirit is still that of a child. He needs to see another child grow up and leave the house to understand his own need to move to a new "home." Jonathan's uncle still feels protective toward the youth and the house: when Jonathan crosses over, his uncle will follow. Both ghosts needed their story revealed, before they could heal and find peace.

Skeptical Advisor: We all have access to the Collective Unconscious, when we are in the proper frame of mind. The people involved in this ghost hunt, including myself, may have simply "tapped in" to a creative expression of the Collective Unconscious—an expression that fit the house, surroundings, and stories we'd been told. On a personal note, this was a very dramatic haunting. My connection with Jonathan was more intimate than any I have had, before or since. I vividly remember standing in that kitchen, with tears streaming down my face, sensing the sadness that must have filled his mother's heart. To this day I feel as if I knew this family as well as if they'd lived next door: consequently, I find it hard to accept that the visions and feelings were generated by an over-active imagination. I have since discovered that historian Anthony Cohen considers this region of New York State to have had several underground railroad locations—stops along the way to Canada and to freedom.

Sudden or Untimely Death Ghosts

People who die young, or in instantaneous unforeseen ways, find the transition from life to death confusing, and consequently get stuck in between. These ghosts tend to react to the afterlife in two typical ways. First, they may try to complete things that they wished for or worked toward in life, hoping to find some closure. The ghost of a child who died soon after birth may, if he or she did not receive a name in life, wanders in search of someone willing to bestow a name. If the ghost succeeds, then it can find eternal rest.

The untimely death ghost may just go about the routine it had in life: this second type of reaction is an act of denial. The spirit hopes to reclaim life by mimicking it, only to discover that this creates a mere shadow of reality, without substance or warmth. These poor souls do not realize that they are dead! Some even refuse to acknowledge death when given irrefutable proof that they are non-corporeal. This makes it very difficult to help these spirits find peace.

Here in Western New York we have many beauti- **The Phantom** *ful old buildings with Victorian ambiance. This fea-* **of the Opera** *ture alone make them picturesque settings, in which* **House** *any spirit would be happy to reside. This seems to be the case for the Lancaster Opera house, constructed in the mid-1890s, and the residence of several ghosts.*

First among them is William, an actor who loved the theater but never achieved the greatness he wished. According to psychics, William doesn't know, or doesn't care, that he's dead. The opera house is also haunted by a lavender-clad woman whose history remains mysterious, and by the confused ghost of a belltower keeper, who had an untimely heart attack while working.

The deceased thespian, William, is by far the most dramatic ghost in residence. He exhibits minor manifestations of poltergeist-type behavior, including opening doors, messing papers, and moving objects; cold rushes of air occasionally hit actors on the stage. A local psychic from the Psychical Research Center has investigated William and declared him harmless.

As for the bellkeeper, about the only report of his activity seems to be that the elevator is intent on going to the third floor—as if the bellkeeper

53

is returning to his duties. Because of the gentle nature of these spirits, no one—to my knowledge—has tried to exorcise the building. Perhaps it's just as well. Somehow the ivory and gold stage, maple and oak wood-work, and horseshoe balcony seem a fitting setting for these three lost souls.

William seems to be a fettered ghost, blissfully unaware of his demise, repeatedly drawn back to the stage that he loved. The bellkeeper is a sudden or untimely death ghost, taking his responsibilities to heart even after death. The lavender woman was likely an actress or ardent supporter of the arts, returning to her seat in the balcony to enjoy the shows.

It is possible to help spirits who suffered a sudden or untimely death toward a new reality. For example, the bellkeeper might move on if he feels the right person has taken over his job.

Skeptical Advisor: Ambiance and local lore can play tricks on our imaginations. The lighting and props of an old theater are designed to have a strong suggestive impact on our senses. Additionally, people visiting such locations often come expecting a supernatural experience, which heightens the likelihood of a "false face."

Unresolved Issue Ghosts

In Buddhist tradition, the spirit of a person can live at a crossroads or boundary near its old home. The being remains as a ghost in this location, until it exhausts the karma of the greed it indulged in during life: then it can move on to a new rebirth. This spirit, a type of *preta*, or "hungry ghost," is an unresolved issue ghost.

Unresolved issue ghosts make up a fairly large majority of disincarnate spirits. To understand why, ask a dozen or so people if they have any regrets, or if they wish they'd done things differently in the past. Such feelings, common among most of us, can become fetters in the afterlife, binding the spirit to complete or refine a specific task.

A spirit can also be fettered to the unresolved issues of a living person. In this case, the ghost needs to clear things up for the living person, and feels compelled to stay until it achieves that goal.

Grandmother's Headstone

I am not a ghost seer, but I had an experience several years ago that made me believe such encounters are a real possibility. I was very close to my maternal grandmother, who promised to give me her wedding rings, worn faithfully for 40 years, upon graduation. While she did not live to see that moment, my mother kept these safe for me, and I have worn them ever since. I believe these rings are what afforded me a connection to my grandmother, and what made her visit possible.

Grandmother died when I was thirteen. My father refused to pay for a headstone for her, which seemed to me a tremendously undeserved insult. Grandmother had been very kind in her life, and now it was as if that didn't matter because mom and dad were divorced. This bothered me for a very long time.

Then, about eight years ago at Halloween, I helped set up an altar for the dead where everyone who gathered could honor their departed ancestors. The centerpiece included a black mirror that, we believe, will allow a person to peer through into the spirit world, across the veil. Everyone brought pictures and items that belonged to their relatives, creating a lovely memorial tribute.

As I went to the altar, I fingered grandmother's rings and thought about her for a moment. My goal was to apologize and let her know she wasn't forgotten. As I looked up, I felt a sense of vertigo and suddenly saw myself enveloped by grandmother's image. She was just as I remembered; her clothes, her hair, her aroma, and even the emotions she generated. Grandma was strong and feisty, as was her spirit.

As I watched in awe, I noticed the most amusing smirk on her face. She waved me off with an amused "phtt" before I heard her voice in my head. She said "Oh, for heaven's sake! I'm not there anyway. Goodness, you worry about silly things. I am fine, having a good time, always here if you need me. Love you." That was it. She was gone, and while it felt like all this transpired over a few moments, more than 45 minutes had passed.

Several years after this, my sister went to a psychic who instructed her to get that headstone so my grandma's angry spirit could rest. Even as my sister shared this, I could still hear grandma's "phtt" in my mind, dismissing the idea as unimportant, at least to her. Nonetheless, my sister got the headstone and held a small Native American style blessing. Grandmother's mental commentary was humorous as before. "Ah, smoke is always good now and then. What silliness, but thanks anyway, girls."

Since these experiences, I have been certain of my grandmother's happiness. This certainty is uncanny and unreasonable, but definitely there for good.

—Colleen

The grandmother's ghost appeared for two reasons—grandmother's desire to watch over and care for her loved ones, and Colleen's unresolved feelings about buying a headstone.

Skeptical Advisor: The psychological issues involved with these types of experience are undeniable. These experiences may be subconscious "answers" to issues that eluded conscious resolution.

If your experiences mirror one or several of the descriptions in this chapter, you may have a ghost on your hands. Now what? Do you leave it alone? Try to help? Whatever your choice, it is good to know as much as possible about your spiritual visitor—or visitors—before doing anything. The next chapter will help you distinguish "False Faces" from ghosts.

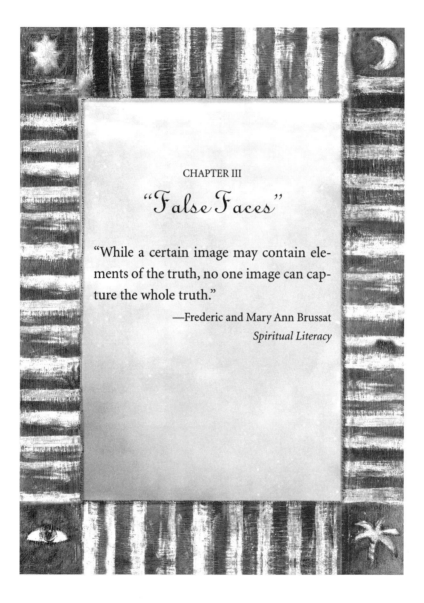

CHAPTER III

"False Faces"

"While a certain image may contain elements of the truth, no one image can capture the whole truth."

—Frederic and Mary Ann Brussat
Spiritual Literacy

Some beings and energies are commonly mistaken for the spirits of the dead. These are "false faces"—none of them are ghosts, but they may not always be easy to distinguish from ghosts. Some "false faces" are beings who interact with humans. The rest are energies—these could be human, or non-human—that don't interact with us; they just put in an appearance. Any sighting or report of "ghostly" activity should be evaluated, to determine whether the apparition is a ghost, or is some other phenomenon.

Angels and Spirit Guides

The word "angel" comes from the Greek *angelos*, which means 'messenger.' Angels are supernatural beings of semi-divine nature, often portrayed as winged and beautiful. Accounts of angelic sightings describe angels as surrounded by light. They project an ambiance that makes them seem approachable, and sometimes appear smiling to put those who behold them at ease.

An angelic presence is not always visible. Some people simply feel the presence of a protective attendant nearby, especially in times of crisis. They might sense, for example, someone acting as a buffer between them and serious injury.

Spirit guides can be anyone from a deceased relative to a master teacher. Their function is, of course, to guide and protect. Like angels, they are not to be feared. Spirit guides and angels come to ward you from harm, to inspire, or to instruct. In almost all cases, they come bearing some type of message from the universe to which you should pay close attention. This message can come in an incredible variety of forms—through a dream, through a sign, or even through telepathic communication.

At first glimpse, an angel and a spirit guide appear similar: both are suffused with light and have protective attributes. And not all angels have wings! Some angels, such as angelic hitchhikers and hoboes, who appear to test one's charity and then disappear—look very ordinary. The main distinction between angels and spirit guides is metaphysical: spirit guides still have to reincarnate to unite with the Divine; angels do not have to reincarnate.

Skeptic Advisor: Angelic imagery can be a mental trick or coping mechanism that offers comfort in times of duress.

Kami

Kami is a Japanese term for spirits who reside in objects and have great magical powers. Kami may be nature spirits or the spirits of great people. The term means "beings who are more highly placed." While such an entity's energies might be mistaken for a ghost, its powers are far greater, comparable to angelic powers. Consequently, treat the Kami with care and respect. If you find yourself uncomfortable with such a spirit, I suggest giving the associated object to another who feels naturally drawn to its energy.

Skeptic Advisor: Kami may be a type of energy imprint, or a memory rather than an actual spirit.

Religious Figures

The ability to see visions of religious figures, saints, Mary, or Christ is considered a Charism—a gift of grace—by the Catholic Church. This ability is one of the signs of sainthood. The Bible, like many sacred texts, speaks of visions that were life-changing: some of these resulted in conversion, some in the awakening of spiritual gifts, some in the dedication of the visionary's life to the ministry.

Ghostly apparitions can also have a transformative effect on our lives: spirits, however, seem to change our views of death, while religious visions change the *way* we live. The religious figures seen in a vision are not true ghosts. While they are spiritual, these powerful presences are not limited to, or trapped in, this world or the next one. They are somewhat like Evolved Ghosts in this regard.

Ghostly monks, nuns, priests, and religious figures are a fascinating sub-group. Despite the human spirit's quest for reunification with the Divine, even the most devout seem to like to linger in this world. Two famous photographs taken in England in the 1940s and '50s are good examples of this kind of haunting. One shows a medieval monk standing prayerfully at the altar of St. Nicholas's Church in Sussex; the other, taken in Kent, reveals a phantom vicar in Eastry Church. The photographs have been reviewed by experts, none of whom found evidence of trick photography.

Skeptical Advisor: Some critics claim that double exposures cause believable-looking phantoms to appear superimposed on the photo's background: the English photos may be a double image, rather spectral imprints from the spirits of a monk and a vicar.

Visionaries usually see religious figures and archetypes from their own culture and religion. Few followers of Buddha report visions of a typical Christian priest. Faith and expectation seems to play an integral role in these manifestations.

Fairies

Prankish creatures who adore playing harmless tricks on unsuspecting humans, fairies may be at work if you keep losing small sparkling items (only to find them some days or months later), or if you hear the slight tinkling of bells and child-like giggles. Fairies are drawn to children and pets first, then to very loving, adventurous, creative adults. If the cat has been chasing empty air, or your two-year-old talks about flying invisible friends, consider the possibility that you have been chosen for a visitation from the fairy folk.

Fairies are an easy lot to contend with. Every few days, go to your window ledge or garden, and leave out a bit of sweet bread, or some heavy cream, ale, bubbly wine, or honey cakes. This should keep them quite content.

If a fairy seems nasty or too roguish for peaceful coexistence, try some of the techniques used to keep ghosts away. Sprinkle salt and iron filings around the home, hang holly year-round, and use a tincture of St. John's Wort on all the doors, windows, and other openings (such as air ducts). You have to let the fairy know who's boss of this territory. None of these measures will hurt the fairy. You have simply deterred it from bothering you. (For more tips on getting rid of ghosts, see the next chapter, "Hauntings," and Appendix A, "Spirit Superstitions.")

Astral Projection

The astral body is composed of etheric energy: the laws of physical matter do not apply to it, so it can traverse long distances in an instant, and move through solid objects unhindered. In the astral state, a person is conscious, alert, and functional—and he is not constrained by the body.

After experiencing an OBE, people report having visited places, family, or friends. They directed their astral body with their thoughts on these journeys. People who receive an astral visit sometimes sense that someone else is there; they may even see a shadowy image. It is, therefore, common to mistake an astral visitor for a ghost.

People who are badly injured, or people in a situation of crisis, can spontaneously project their spirit into the presence of someone they were thinking about, or of someone they care about. This is a typical feature of astral visits, and may explain the visions seen by families and friends of the dying. Sometimes these visits announce the moment of death to the distant loved ones.

Just prior to my father's death, my four-year-old **Grandpa Feels** *son came running down the stairs shaking, visibly* **Much Better** *upset. "Grandpa's gone!" he exclaimed, adding "but* **Now** *he said he feels much better now." This statement was particularly startling since we had not discussed my father's condition with Karl—*

and only moments later we received a call from the hospital, confirming my father's death. Throughout that day Karl reiterated the message given to him by the vision in his room to everyone who would listen. At the moment between life and death, dad's spirit projected to his namesake—Karl. This gave the family peace of mind.

If Karl's grandfather had not experienced the trauma of passage that night, I don't know if Karl would have seen anything or received a message. At the moment that vision occurred it was not, as yet, generated by a ghost.

Skeptical Advisor: Astral projection may be mimicked by a flying dream, as can images of those we hold dear.

Near-Death Projections
During Near-Death Experiences, the spirit can separate from the body. It is not a ghost, and many cultures recognized this by giving the NDE spectral figure a distinctive name. The Fetch (Old English), the Doppelganger (German), and the Vardger (Norse) are all designations that remind us that NDE apparitions are not an innovation of the "New Age."

NDE projections can communicate with the living, by some accounts. The story above, where a young child intercepted an NDE projection from his grandfather, describes a classic NDE communication. These visits are typically attempts to resolve issues with the living, or to say final farewells to people with close emotional ties.

If the person projecting the NDE specter dies before the message gets across, this might result in a haunting, centered around the person the specter intended to visit. This sort of ghost will likely move on once it feels that its message has been received and understood.

Skeptical Advisor: The NDE specter may represent some type of latent telepathy that produces visual images. Just as you can know that a friend is in trouble, even though you haven't heard from them, strong emotional ties create instinctive warning systems. Our reactions to this instinctive alarm will vary: some people might see a "spirit."

The unusual sensations associated with NDEs—flying, floating, memory flashbacks, seeing the body from outside—may be due to oxygen deprivation to the brain.

Poltergeists

The German word *"poltergeist"* refers to a roaring or noisy spirit. Poltergeist activity—a series of clamorous events in an area—is sometimes blamed on ghosts, sometimes on other sorts of spirits.

Poltergeists have a long and distinguished history. One of the first poltergeist accounts comes from the first-century Roman historian Livy, who described people being battered by stones thrown by an unseen source. In the twelfth century, the scholar Gerald of Wales mentioned an aggressive spirit which threw mud and cut up clothing. During the Middle Ages, it was believed that poltergeists were demons; during the Reformation, reports of a poltergeist resulted in a witch hunt. The notion that witches instigated poltergeist activity continued well into the eighteenth century. It seems to have been due to the fact that poltergeist phenomena usually centered around young women.

Modern surveys indicate that poltergeist activity usually lasts a few weeks, but that some persistent cases continue for a year. Besides being noisy, poltergeists snatch, move, or toss about small objects. Bottles sometimes pop open, or items float through the air. Less commonly, poltergeists cause water leaks, ignite fires, pinch or make other sorts of physical contact, write on walls, vandalize property, materialize objects, commit violence, or manifest strong odors. The poltergeist seems to center itself on a person, following him or her from place to place.

Skeptical Advisor: Poltergeist activity rarely occurs without the focal person nearby. Women under twenty, exhibiting signs of emotional distress, are much more likely than other people to experience this phenomenon. This has given rise to the contemporary theory that a poltergeist is actually a psychically projected scourge of someone unable or unwilling to express inner conflict. This is called "recurrent spontaneous psychokinesis."

Phantom Beasts
Mythical beasts are a little difficult to explain: what are they doing in the modern landscape? These could be alive; but, if a particular creature once roamed the earth as a living being, it may have left a ghost. Here is one such story.

While honeymooning in Scotland, we traveled to the Island of Lewis in the Hebrides. Three sets of standing stones remain here, all of which sur-rounded the small cottage where we stayed. Late in the afternoon, after the tourist busses left, we went exploring the large central circle of stones, and the heathered knoll just beyond, which looked out over the ocean.

Of Heathered Hills and Dragon's Lair

As we approached the hill, everything seemed quite normal—until we stepped on the mound. The sheep stopped braying, birds stopped singing, and silence fell around us like a damp cloth. It was like walk-ing on hallowed ground, and we obviously weren't welcome. So we quickly retreated, and the animals immediately went back about their business. The exact meaning of this experience would not come into fo-cus until late that night, and on the following day.

We woke well past midnight to see a fire blazing at the main set of stones. We could overhear our hosts in a neighboring room, whispering quietly in Gaelic. As we watched, a dark figure appeared on top of the center stone. It was huge and winged, with a face and figure betraying its dragon nature. The beast flew into the air, circled the standing stones thrice, then moved on. We quickly returned to the safety of bed, not at all certain that our imaginations weren't getting out of control.

The next day we took the Stornoway Ferry back to the mainland. On the boat, an old man was telling a young boy about the Dragon of Myrddin, a great beast who guards the standing stones. According to the legend this man retold, the creature comes out periodically, to look af-ter the stones and their keepers. Needless to say, we were anxious to hear more in the wake of our own experiences: we deboarded early, in hopes of meeting the elderly man. Neither he nor the young boy ever emerged from the ship, and no other passengers remember seeing them.

Skeptical Advisor: In this story, the young boy and the grandfatherly figure could have been ghosts of the region. The image of the dragon remains a mystery. Has this legend been held in communal regard for so long that it became a thought-form? Is the creature a manifestation of our ancestral memory of flying dinosaurs? Did the beast exist once, and does it now continue its duties from beyond the grave?

Phantom Buildings

Ghostly buildings are probably imposters, energy imprints created by a communal or cultural mind. A person coming home, unaware that a regional landmark has suddenly burned down, might still see a shadowy image of the landmark. Remaining on that same spot for decades or centuries, that building may have left its image imprinted on the skyline, across the land, and in people's minds. Unless other bodily images accompany the building, this isn't a haunting in the true sense.

Auric Emanations

All living things produce energy in some form. Even non-living things, like quartz crystal, have the capacity to collect and transmit energy. The aura is one type of energy emanation, and visionaries have described and depicted it for thousands of years.

In the *History of Magic,* the nineteenth-century occultist Eliphas

Levi wrote that the highest principle was light, "the vibrations of which are the movement of life and all things." In the *Encyclopedia of the Occult*, Lewis Spence defines the aura as a "cloud of light suffused with various colors." Medieval artists painted haloes, Paracelsus described the "fiery glove" of the aura," and St. Philip of Neri described the "envelope of light" that surrounds the body.

The human aura, then, is the body's atmosphere, within which personal energy is suspended. Animals and plants also have auras. The physical being is a nucleus, surrounded by the aura and, in turn, holding it in place. When you perceive this energy, what you see depends on two factors—the nature of the being at its nucleus, and the state you are in.

Many observers would see a glow behind, or beside, a particularly outgoing person standing in a darkened doorway, Some might think they had seen a ghost; others would know that they had seen the auric field. A person with a latent ability to see the light of an aura may catch it in his peripheral vision, but the images are so fleeting that they may seem to be spirits appearing and disappearing.

Cumulative Energy

Any area that has been inhabited, or visited regularly, collects energies from all the people who have frequented it. Houses and apartments especially gather this energy together: this makes up the ambiance or personality of the home. This personality usually goes unnoticed: most people just sense a slight mood that seems natural. In some cases the energy becomes a distinct and demanding thought-form that might be mistaken for a poltergeist, or some other ghostly resident.

This House Wants Children! *When I first looked at the house in which we live now, I was struck by how spiritually clean it seemed, for a residence bordering on 200 years old. There was just one lingering spirit—an old woman—who was quite content to stay in her room; one haunted piece of furniture; and one negative memory area that was quickly abated by fresh paint and a little TLC. Nonetheless, something was terribly wrong here. The house itself was very unhappy.*

After we moved in, I found out why. There, lovingly laid out in a scrapbook in the attic, were pictures of former residents, their children, their pets, and all the structural changes that happened in the house over the past two centuries. The former owners of the house were childless, and had made no renovations in a decade. The house's established family energies did not like their lifestyle one bit, and seemed quite relieved to have us—with our son, four cats, and a dog—taking over and renovating.

Not surprisingly, about two months later I was pregnant with a second child. To this day I believe the house wanted more children, and my husband and I felt that desire.

To anyone who didn't know better, all these odd feelings might have been chalked up to a restless, malcontent spirit. Cumulative energy is, however, merely a haunt-like phenomenon; it is also relatively easy to cure. First, recognize that these energies are most evident during times of drastic change. If you've just moved in and everything seems out of kilter, this awkwardness may disappear naturally, with time and redecoration.

If the problem does not abate, be sensitive to your home's energy patterns. In other words, if your walls can talk, what are they trying to tell you? I remember going to move an antique mirrored table from one area in my entryway to another, when I suddenly felt as though I'd hurt someone's feelings. So the table stayed where it was, and remains there to this day, as my way of honoring the house's history. A friend of mine uses an ever-burning candle to represent the house's thought-form, and the new energy her family brings to it each day.

Finally, if you find the home's personality is simply incompatible with your own, you may have to put your foot down in some manner, and claim your space. One such story follows.

The Upstart Spirit

When I moved into my home, the residing cumulative energy was not happy. One family had lived in the house for nearly seventy years. Their lifestyle was drastically different from mine, and the residual thought-form didn't like this change one bit. So, it tried to inspire certain fitting behaviors in me. I found myself vehemently cleaning, nearly to the point of neurosis. Worse, guests who were normally gentle, loving people would find themselves gossiping self-righteously, like some sort of select social club!

I tried numerous ways of communicating with the house, letting it know this behavior was unacceptable, but it didn't work. Finally, in desperation I blessed the house with a mixture of bourbon and cigarette ashes, followed by an end-to-end romp with neighborhood children. As unorthodox as this purging may seem, it worked. My cleaning frenzy subsided and my friends were their old selves again. Without a little forceful nudge to make my energy pattern known in no uncertain terms to the house, I'd still be polishing.

—Dorothy

Energy Imprints

Psychics who investigate reports of hauntings distinguish actual spirits from energy imprints. The energy imprint is a kind of residual force from one specific source: it replays itself like a video recording. There are reports of visions in which a violent act is replayed on the anniversary of its occurrence. While this replay may include ghostly figures, this is just a spectral history: no real personality or substance is at work.

The major difference between an imprint and the thought-form of cumulative energy is this: an imprint is totally unaware of human existence, or anything else. Over time the image may disperse, or be overlaid by other imprints. Few people have had much success with attempts to dissipate this phenomenon by force. Because the impression does not respond to the mundane world—as a ghost or thought-form does—it is difficult to break its cycle of repetition.

Psychic Phenomena

People who are unaware of their psychic abilities might mistake the manifestation of these talents for a ghostly presence. For example, someone who has clairaudience—the ability to hear sounds or words that are not within our normal range of awareness—may suspect that they heard the whispering of ghosts. If someone has a propensity for telekinesis and happens to move an object unwittingly, he or she could think the movement was the work of a spirit. Children especially exhibit such abilities. Before my son Karl could walk, he displayed telekinetic abilities with a candle shaped like a magician, and with his pacifier. The image of a pacifier floating in midair was startling, to say the least. If I had not seen him gesturing to these items just moments before they moved, I might have wondered if a ghost or poltergeist was in the house.

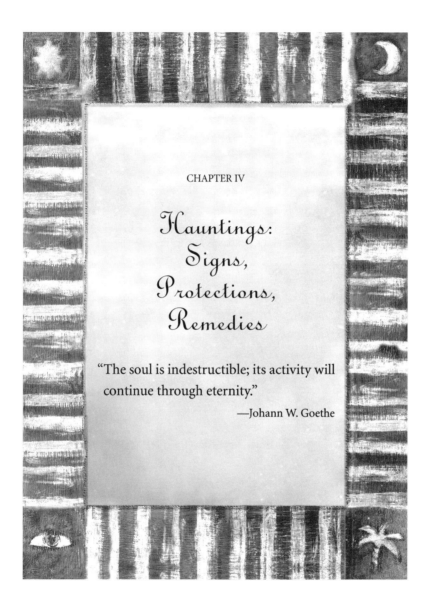

CHAPTER IV

Hauntings:
Signs,
Protections,
Remedies

"The soul is indestructible; its activity will
continue through eternity."

—Johann W. Goethe

How do we know that a house, area, or object is haunted? It's not easy. There can be natural causes for the events and activities reported in a haunting. Swamp gas and floaters might explain an odd visual image. Wind, a settling house, or a playful pet may be responsible for spooky noises. Or the spiritual entity you encounter may be one of the "false faces" we looked at in the previous chapter. So what's a layperson ghost hunter to do?

When you first suspect the presence of a ghost, begin immediately to maintain detailed records. Later on, these may help verify or disprove a haunting, with the aid of experts. Records should include the following entries.

(Date, time, and duration of each incident, along with a detailed description of what happened.
(Sound recordings, photographs, or video recordings, if the equipment is available.
(A description of the prevalent environmental factors, including the weather, and any people or pets present.
(Names and addresses of any witnesses, and their own narratives of what they experienced.

Remember what you have learned about ghosts and energy emanations—their kinds and their behavior. Since the differences between ghosts and "false faces" can be minimal, you will need to sharpen your perception to notice these. Extend and hone your physical, mental, and spiritual senses.

If you cherish specific expectations, these may create a self-in-duced experience. Suppose a child is afraid that monsters lurk in the dark. Upon going to bed, the child is likely to think he or she sees one in the shadows, or to dream of monsters. Adults are not immune to such imaginings. One night, after reading about ghosts, I looked into a darkened room—and saw an odd, etheric glow. My heart began to race, and I tried desperately to find my camera. But I found, when I examined the room closely, that the glow came from moonlight, re-flecting off a crystal on the windowsill. Skepticism is your ally when you catalogue apparently ghostly phenomena.

Indications That a Home or Object Is Haunted

Objects or homes can be haunted by a spirit attached to them. A ghost can develop a very strong emotional attachment to a place, or an item—usually one it owned or coveted during life. When the attach-ment is so intense that it hinders a spirit's transition into the next life, the object is called a "fetter." You can tell whether there is a fetter by ex-amining the symptoms the environment or object exhibits.

To help you refine your investigation, I have provided a list of common symptoms of hauntings. These entries will help you deter-mine whether you are dealing with a *ghost*. A "false face," or a natu-ral phenomenon, will exhibit different symptoms, which are discussed in the "Skeptical Advisor" sections.

Aroma

Distinct scents wafting through the home—with no apparent source—are one telltale sign of a haunt. You may smell a spirit's favorite food, flower, perfume, or cologne. Ghosts can cause unpleasant scents, too—hot tar or cigar smoke, for instance. Please remember that nasty smells do not necessarily indicate that the *ghost* is nasty. The scent is simply a trademark for the deceased person. Maybe your ghost was a street engineer, or a cigar smoker.

The aroma in a room may represent some notable event in the ghost's earthly life. Let's suppose that you recently cleaned the cellar, but it suddenly begins smelling very damp and musty. The smell could be a sign that a flood occurred here, some time in the past. A ghost may have lived through that flood or died in it.

Skeptical Advisor: The smell could also be a scented energy imprint, rather than the work of a ghost. When you investigate any strange aroma, check within and around the area to determine if it has a natural cause. Look around, determine which way the wind is blowing, and find out what types of buildings and plants are nearby. Check the pets and children for possible influences. Such detailed measures are important in all your ghost hunting!

Children and Pets

Children and animals are more sensitive to the presence of spirits than adults are. We need to pay more attention to their instincts, especially when we investigate hauntings. The following story is a case in point.

The Haunted Sewing Machine

I was moving some furniture around in my house, bringing an antique pedal sewing machine down from the attic. I stopped and left the machine on the landing to take a breather: at this point, my Keeshond started to bark wildly. He sat at the bottom of the stairs, looking intently at the machine, and would not stop barking until I moved it off the landing into the living room. Even then, the dog walked cautiously around the machine. It took a week for this behavior to wane. I believe this reaction was caused by a spirit attached to the machine, although I was oblivious to its presence.

The ancients regarded dogs as having a special gift—dogs could sense spirits. Certain animals—birds, for instance—may actually carry a spirit with them. Babies have free access to the spirit realms for a period just after they are born, because their crown chakra—located at the top of the head, where an infant has a "soft spot"—is open. Children are also more sensitive than adults, because children do not have as many conditioned responses to hinder or prejudice their perceptions.

So, if a child talks of a friend you can't see, get a description and listen closely to your child. If your pets take notice of something, and you see nothing, get ready: you may find yourself playing with that "nothing," or running from it, should it turn out to be a ghost.

Skeptical Advisor: Animals have a different range of hearing, smell, and vision than we do: they could be reacting to environmental causes, rather than ghosts. Children have rich imaginations, which are easily influenced by books and other media.

Disappearing, Reappearing, or Rearranged Items

My roommate and I used to live with a spirit who delighted in straightening pictures and messing closets. The spirit would get busier whenever there was a lot of human activity in the house—numerous guests coming and going, or intense spring cleaning sessions. I have received descriptions of similar hauntings, in which books or jewelry disappear, only to reappear in unexpected places.

Try to determine why a spirit wants to rearrange or remove items. Taking jewelry or a book may be a way for it to feel closer to this world. A ghost who frequently throws cards around may have a moral taboo against card playing.

Skeptical Advisor: Did you move the suspect item yourself? You may not have been conscious of doing so. A playful pet or fairy may have moved it. In regions prone to tremors, objects are more likely to be displaced. Check whether the area is prone to drafts, or gusts of wind—especially if you are trying to account for lightweight items like playing cards.

Dreams

Dreaming is honored and given great importance in many cultures. For Australian Aborigines, dreaming is the time when the living can commune with spirits, the ancestors, and the gods. In cultures as distant as Greece, Japan, and Germany, dreaming was regarded as a way to release the mind from its usual constraints, and to open it to new potential, including an awareness of a haunting.

The Greeks called the god of dreams Morpheus: he was the son of Hypnos ("Sleep") and a cousin to Thanatos ("Death"). Sleep and dream were states that had a unique connection to the afterlife and to the spirits that dwelt there. The connection was so strong that the Greeks believed that the people closest to death were also the best and most dependable dream oracles!

In ancient Japan, the Emperor was the official dreamer for his people. He would go into seclusion to commune with the supernatural world through his dreams. Upon waking, he would communicate these messages to his staff and the community.

In Germanic regions, people once believed that spirits who visited during sleep brought them luck and protection. Usually these spirits were female; they may have been a communal expression of the fertility goddess, or fate, in that culture.

The idea that sleepers could receive communications from spirits of the dead continued through the Renaissance. In the sixteenth century, the Swiss mystic and physician Paracelsus wrote that dreaming of people who had been dead for more than fifty years was one way to receive knowledge from the next world.

Poets as well as historians have recognized the connection between sleep, death, and dreams. Shakespeare's Hamlet concluded that suicide would not extinguish his consciousness, "for in that sleep of death what dreams may come." As early as 720 B.C., the Greek historian Hesiod spoke of sleep as the brother of death.

Sleep, death, and dreams are connected within the human consciousness; our dream time, then, can become like an inter-dimensional modem that intercepts and interprets messages from dimensions other than the waking world. While we sleep, our mind is less busy with mundane thoughts, so there is time and opportunity to access normally untapped portions of gray matter. We use about 30 percent of our brain's total capacity daily: what happens when someone opens the doorway to even five percent more? I believe that people who access these unexercised portions of their brains are those who have psychic abilities.

Dream apparitions usually deal with someone very close to the dreamer. A ghost haunting a residence may try this avenue of communication, if it has a story to tell, or an unresolved issue. Such ghosts may look for any available, open-minded person. If you begin having dream encounters with a ghost, make detailed notes of anything it tells you, and of any recurrent scenarios. After a while, patterns should develop within your data. You can then check these against historical records, to determine what the ghost is trying to describe.

> *Skeptical Advisor:* Our mind has a vast capacity to store information. During sleep, subconscious knowledge—such as regional history—can become available to us. Dreams are largely subjective: their content cannot be authenticated by anyone other than the dreamer.

Fire Signs

The human spirit has often been compared to a spark or flame. Fire, by association, is thought to behave oddly in the presence of spirits. There are many bits of lore about the behavior of fire. A blue flame, for example, indicates the presence of a ghost. A "winding sheet"—a long twirl of wax on one side of a candle—can mean that a ghost is in the vicinity (although it has also been taken as a sign that a living person is about to cross over to the afterlife). A fire that burns brightly on one side, but barely at all on the other, has a ghost standing nearby. The flames are quenched by cold winds from the world of the dead.

Skeptical Advisor: The flow of candle wax is easily influenced by wind, or by the physical structure of the candle. Wood may burn oddly due to a breeze or to dampness; a fire can be blown out by a downdraft.

Mood and Ambiance

The ambiance of a region or house is strongly associated with energy impressions and cumulative energy. If this ambiance is extremely specific and potent, you may have a ghost present. Have you ever walked into an unfamiliar place and felt totally uncomfortable with it? Your feeling may be due to the presence of an unhappy spirit, or to negative energy imprints.

Skeptical Advisor: Feelings of comfort and discomfort are subjective: they may simply be due to your level of self-confidence. Your impressions of a place can be subconsciously shaped by any information you heard about it, prior to visiting. If you were told the place was haunted, you will go into it expecting a spooky feeling.

Noises

Footsteps, cupboards opening, windows closing, objects dragging—these noises are often reported as part of a haunting. A ghost may be attempting to tell a story with these noises. If the ghost always sat in a favorite rocking chair, for example, the sound of creaking floorboards might occur. If the ghost paced the floor waiting for errant children, footsteps might be heard. Knowing that ghosts use noises to communicate, Victorian sensitives often brought drums or tambourines to their séances. The instrument was set on a table so that the ghost's vibrations could set it off. Unfortunately, wiggling an elbow at an apt moment could imitate this effect.

In 1959, the Swedish film producer Friedrich Jurgenson captured the voices of the dead on a tape recorder. Interested in his results, a group of engineers and independent scientists attempted regulated experiments in the 1970s: these yielded numerous taped voices in a variety of languages. These became known as electronic voice phenomena (EVP). Other investigations ensued, some of which seemed to prove or disprove EVP.

Skeptical Advisor: If you hear odd noises, check for pets, children, mice, wind-sensitive items, loose boards, or rattling shutters, before you reach for your ghost-banishing guide. Even music boxes can sound suddenly, if a spring loosens over time.

Physical Manifestations

Physical manifestations—incidents when a living person is brushed against by a ghost, or feels its touch—are rare. Touch is an intimate sense. Unless you are very open and sensitive to the spirit realm, you are unlikely to experience this. A ghost would have to exert tremendous energy in order to cause physical sensations in a living person.

Ghost of Christmas Present *On the day after the anniversary of my father's death, my son came running downstairs, crying and visibly shaken. When asked what was wrong, he said that he woke to find grandpa in bed with him, but thought it was Santa Claus! After drying his tears and allaying his fears, I went to a private spot and had a heart-to-heart with my dad, explaining the inappropriateness of physical manifestations to children. Somehow the message got through. From that point forward he only appeared in my son's dreams.*

Skeptical Advisor: Muscle twitches, nerves firing, and even a light breeze can mimic a ghostly physical manifestation. Shiatsu practitioners and other touch therapists believe that our body remembers everything that happens to us, and that physical touch can release those memories. A touch in the right place may free up a buried memory; that memory may in turn be mistaken for a ghostly experience.

Temperature Changes

The temperature of a haunted area may shift up or down, but experience teaches that it is most likely to drop down. We tend to associate coldness with the absence of life, so the effect may be partly psychological. We tend to "translate" an encounter with lifeless energy into a feeling of physical coldness. Hot spots, by the way, seem to happen where there has been a fire in the past, or where there is a very angry spirit.

Skeptical Advisor: Check for open windows, fans, refrigerators, and weather conditions that could cause the change in temperature. Ley lines, which are manifestations of the earth's aura, can cause false hot spots of a less dramatic nature. Increased energy along a ley line warms up the area. Hot spots can also be mimicked by a heating system with odd cracks in the ducts and similar mechanical objects.

Visual Manifestations

The stereotypical ghost is wispy and shadowy, but in fact many ghosts are so solid that we mistake them for people. Most of us do not realize that we saw a ghost until it has faded away or walked through a wall! Most of us catch glimpses at random, and it is difficult to explain why or how. If our subconscious has a way to detect the presence of stranded souls and other spirits, it could then interpret them visually. It is a mysterious ability: psychics and clairvoyant mediums do have a knack for seeing ghosts, but may not be able to explain the mechanics of how they do it.

The camera can sometimes capture a visual manifestation. I have found startling images in snapshots I took in Scotland: one of a silvery-blue helmet on a bench in front of a castle; and another of pink and purple light in the shape of a woman's figure, standing near the headstone at Callanish. I had no intentions of capturing "ghosts" when I took these pictures, and they came from different rolls of film.

Skeptical Advisor: Floaters, odd light reflections, after-images caused by bright light or constant color stimulus, and unexpected memories all cause visual images that might be mistaken for ghosts. Review the environment for possible causes, and check your eyeglasses for smudges. A fogged lens, a random insect flying through the picture, double exposures, reflections, and technical problems can all cause imposters on developed film.

Winds

Wind and air, like spirits, are invisible and elusive. Some early schools of Greek philosophy thought that the wind contained the World-Soul. Greek religion assigned a god to each of the winds that blew from the four directions. Many cultures believe that the spirit is a subtle wind inside the body, and that it leaves the body with the last breath.

A breeze suddenly appearing or disappearing, with no discernible cause, might be a sign that a ghost or spirit has come—or gone. The intensity of the wind and its demeanor can be read for signs of the spirit's mood—a harsh, destructive wind may be caused by an angry ghost. Most ghost winds are cold. Some winds waft the ghost's trademark aroma through the area.

Skeptical Advisor: Check the chimney flues and windows. A spirit wind blowing outdoors will be hard to document! But the weather service will have records of unusual wind shears or patterns: check with the local bureau to see if they know of any freak high winds occurring in the vicinity at that time.

Protection from Haunting

Say you're moving into a new residence. How can you make sure the house, and its contents, are a spirit-free zone? Some ghosts are so quiet that you may only sense their existence on the farthest reaches of your awareness. So the first step in protecting yourself from spirits is becoming more aware of them.

Learning to extend your senses into other realities takes time and practice. We are used to interpreting the world in very concrete terms. Expanded sensory perception requires that we believe there is something beyond our awareness to discover. We must also start to trust the instincts we once dismissed as "just a feeling." To help develop augmented awareness, I give my students two exercises.

For the first exercise, I ask them to pay special attention to gut feelings and intuitive impulses for an entire year. They take notes of these, and review their diaries once a month, to see how often their intuitions were correct. People are often amazed at how insightful they can be once they start paying attention to their inner voice.

For the second exercise, I have pairs of students team up, to increase their understanding of, and sensitivity to, auric energy. (This is important because a ghost is made up of auric energy.) First, the students burn bay, mint, and rose incense to heighten spiritual senses, and place amethyst in their pockets. According to folklore, this stone increases one's ability to tap into the psychic realm. Next, the two students sit about one foot apart with hands held up, palms facing their partners'. At first the hands nearly touch. As the individuals begin to sense energy dancing between their palms, sometimes feeling it as increased warmth, they visualize it as a glowing ball. They slowly move their hands apart, letting the ball grow. When the sphere is about eight inches in diameter, the exercise turns into a game of energy catch—the sphere is projected back and forth between the two student's auras.

Those who become adept at this exercise find their awareness increases: they notice more acutely the subtle energies in objects and other people. They will then often know if a house or object is haunted: this allows them to stay in control and decide consciously whether to work with, or avoid, a ghostly presence.

I also teach my students the "Three-F Guide" for protecting themselves from ghosts—you can learn this, too. Carry the knowledge of the Three Fs—Faith, Fear, and Folklore—into the field with you.

Faith is indispensable: any protective measure you take against ghosts will be worthless if you don't believe in its effectiveness. A devout Christian may trust in holy water as an effective safeguard, but a Buddhist may not.

Fear is used against you by some spirits—especially malevolent ghosts. Never let your apprehensions about the unknown get the best of you. Know your power as a living soul. If you can overcome fear, you can usually overcome the presence bothering you. You are an independent spirit with free will. No entity has the right to interfere with your personal space. Even so, some spirits try to encroach, desperately or ignorantly: these must be told their place in no uncertain terms. In my home I have a "knock first" policy. This means that any spirit who wants to drop in has to announce his intention like anyone else. Any ghost or spirit who does not do so is politely but firmly asked to leave, using whatever expulsion method is available to me. Remember that if fear and apprehension are not eliminated the attempt at banishing may fail.

Folklore and superstition about ghosts is full of practical tips to prevent hauntings and banish wandering spirits. An abbreviated list of this wonderfully rich tradition is given below. Remember to supplement your personal folklore list with traditions you choose from your own culture—or your own family. Personalized approaches always prove more effective because we relate to them intimately and trust in them on all levels of experience.

(Hindu tradition recommends carrying coral as a protective talisman against evil spirits.
(Place a piece of the herb broom under your pillow to keep away ghosts and the bad dreams caused by spirits. This according to Rumanian tradition.
(Salt has cleansing protective qualities. Moroccans carry it as a ward against hauntings, and rural Americans tossed it on the butter churn to expel malevolent spirits.
(Many South American and South African tribal cultures use noisy instruments, like drums, to scare away any spirits whose presence is detrimental to the region, such as a sickness spirit or a drought spirit.

- Hang rowan wood in the form of a sacred symbol over the door, and place iron pieces beneath the threshold. This measure also keeps out fairies and other elemental spirits.
- Leave a quartz crystal in an object or room that seems haunted. According to Chinese belief, this stone keeps ghosts content.
- The Victorians created a decorative item called charm wands to keep their homes safe from random or malevolent spirits. To make your own: fill a clear tube to capacity with tiny seeds or beans, then cap it. Hang it near your door. The spirit must count the seeds before it enters your house; this takes all night, however, and the rising sun drives it away.
- Among the Anglo-Saxons, bundles of garlic and rosemary or hot cross buns made on Easter (spring equinox) were hung in homes as a safeguard from spirits. The garlic also banished the undead. Shellac your hot cross buns for longevity—and so they don't attract unwanted insects.
- To discharge a spirit who visits a home or object often, turn all the mirrors around, or change a door's location. This will turn the spirit away, or confuse it into leaving.
- In the Middle Ages people used angelica to keep ghosts away. Baneful spirits could be expelled by fennel. Agrimony or fennel can be grown easily in your garden or window boxes.
- The ringing of church bells frightens away devilish spirits.

For more spirit superstitions, consult Appendix A of this book.

Remedying a Haunted Home or Object

If—after all your examination, deductive reasoning, and protective measures—you conclude that a ghost is present, you must decide what to do about it. One strategy is to do nothing at all. If the ghost isn't troublesome, you can decide to leave well enough alone and share the space peacefully. Many people, including fantasy author Katherine Kurtz, find it quite easy and enjoyable to live with their ghosts. This does mean that you must sometimes accommodate a spirit's preferences—leaving an object where the ghost likes it to stay, for instance. But that is the consideration you would naturally show to any resident of your home. Respect your specter's space, and it will often return the favor.

Hauntings that interrupt your sleep or personal life, or that scare children, call for action. Try simple and subtle banishings first before calling on a minister or resorting to more drastic measures. For example, your first approach could be to paint and thoroughly clean the affected area or object. While you do so, bless it in some manner appropriate to your faith. Do this as part of your weekly routine.

You may also consider burning cleansing herbs—such as sage, cedar, pine, and frankincense. These aromatics are associated with rites for the dead, and many psychics include them in purgative procedures. Local cooperatives or New Age stores stock aromatics like these, in oil form. Dab the oil on your doorways and windows to mark your personal space—but first make sure that you're not allergic to the scent.

When banishing a spirit, always move counterclockwise around the affected area or object. When blessing the space, move clockwise.

You may also add inspirational music, or any other personal touches you find meaningful.

If an undesired ghost has a specific personality (see "The Upstart Spirit" in the previous chapter), take measures that run counter to its tendencies. If the spirit is somber and gloomy, open all the curtains, turn on all the lights, and rent a bundle of comedy tapes to watch. Meanwhile, enact suitable purifying measures.

Purifying techniques vary according to religion and culture. Some people pray while making sacred signs, while others plant blessed crystals, iron filings, and salt around their home. Invoking a guardian spirit or divine being may remedy the situation. Some people also try to talk directly to the ghost, and to reason with it. The next chapter explains how this is done.

Learn as much as possible about the region or object that seems haunted. If historical records are available, they may provide important clues to the spirit's identity and to why it has not crossed over. Knowing the ghost's story often solves at least half, if not all, of the problems associated with a haunting: Story Ghosts were waiting only for this.

These banishing measures probably won't eliminate energy imprints, unresolved issue ghosts, or spirits who simply don't care that they're dead. In such cases, you may wish to enlist the aid of an expert, or try to communicate directly with the spirit if no help is available. One word of caution: I recommend you find experienced help, even if it takes you a while. Not all spirits are nice, nor do all of them wish to move on to another residence or existence. This makes amateur ghost-banishing a risky endeavor, best handled with caution.

*One of the rooms in my house always seemed a bit
odd to me. This wasn't an overly bad feeling, but it
had an undertone of sadness from a presence I
sensed was female and elderly. I investigated, and was told by neighbors
that several elderly people lived in the house during the depression. A
woman had occupied that room and always sat in a rocking chair near
the window, looking out on the houses and gardens nearby. When I
heard this tale, I moved one of my rocking chairs to that window, and
immediately felt the sadness lift. The lady is still there, but she's happy,
and I see no reason to try to make her leave.*

Fetter hauntings like the one described here are easier to remedy
than traditional hauntings. You need only move the fetter to a location the spirit likes. Finding that location may require several tries.
When you hit on the right location, it feels like putting the last piece
in a puzzle. The ghost, contented, will calm down immediately. If it
is not possible to relocate the object within the home, consider leaving the object at the ghost's grave or with its relatives.

It may turn out to be easier—and more adventurous—to live
with your ghosts. An experience with a ghost inevitably changes
your feelings toward the afterlife, and this life. These encounters remind us to do all we can today, to make our transition to the afterlife smooth. That entails resolving our issues, communicating with
family and friends, leaving the past behind, and looking hopefully
toward tomorrow—a tomorrow where our spirits can return to oneness with the earth, with each other, and with the universe.

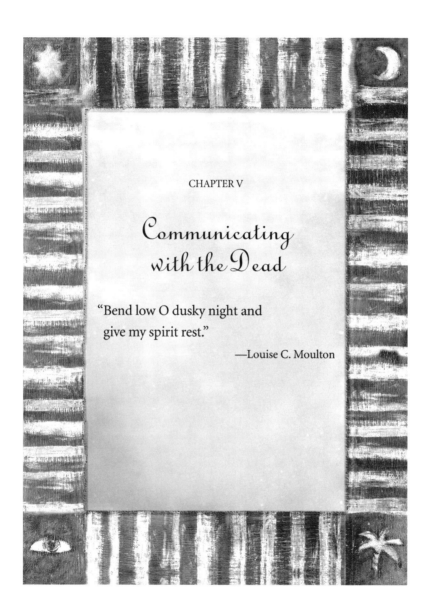

CHAPTER V

Communicating with the Dead

"Bend low O dusky night and
give my spirit rest."

—Louise C. Moulton

We are not the first people to wonder about the afterlife, or seek some assurance that human consciousness will survive the grave. Some hearty folk sought this assurance by visiting sites known to have ghostly inhabitants. Here they hoped to experience something super-normal that would increase their faith. Others, including students of the occult, turned to ceremonies and methodologies that would allow them, from any location, to contact the dead.

One cannot help but wonder what the spirits think of this odd dance, performed by the living, around the subject of mortality and the afterlife. From the astral perspective, this unpartnered waltz might seem evasive. Does it ever answer the question of what awaits the living when they cross beyond? Nonetheless, true to human tenacity, we keep trying!

Conjured Communications

Techniques for contacting spirits still survive from several ancient cultures. Ritual communication with spirits was performed for one of three reasons: to ask the spirit what it knew about the future fortunes of the living; to enlist a spirit's aid for a specific task; and to determine the reason for a ghost's presence. For instance, necromancy, in which spirits are summoned to predict the future or to explain current circumstances, is an ancient science. It was practiced in Mesopotamia and pre-Hellenic Greece. And, until the third century A.D., some early Christian churches allowed communication with the dead.

Our ancestors seemed to feel that the dead had a better perspective about the present and the future. They also believed that these spirits represented a source of energy that could be collected and directed. The Central American sacred text *Popol Vuh* illustrates this outlook. It details ritual procedures for contacting the Land of Shadow. Using these rites, people summoned a spirit's power and captured it in a crystal or fetish for various purposes.

The work of contacting spirits used to be entrusted to a priest, shaman, or other holy person. Such rituals were serious business. If something went wrong, a summoned spirit could get loose and possess a body, or cause terrible troubles like storms or blights. This is why High Magical texts contain precise instructions and severe warnings regarding summoning procedures.

Despite the seemingly dangerous nature, the mystical art of spirit summoning was the basis for an enduring religious system—Spiritualism. In the 1840s, two teenage girls—the Fox sisters—exhibited purported unique psychic abilities, which manifested in clickings and rappings that resembled poltergeist activity. Despite later investigations that showed fraud, the Fox sisters began a wave of enthusiasm for the mystical, which continues to this day. Accounts of the Fox sisters' experiences, and their public displays, led to the founding of the Spiritualist Church, and other metaphysically centered traditions that contribute to the New Age movement.

Spiritualists trust in the ability of the living to communicate with the dead, and in the benefits of doing so. Fundamental tenets of Spiritualism include the ministry of angels, compensation and retribution in the next life for one's actions on earth, and the eternal progression of the soul. Among its past members, Spiritualism can boast of such prominent figures as Victor Hugo and Sir Arthur Conan Doyle.

Mediumship remains the main way that Spiritualists communicate with the dead. Other methods have come into the public eye, including channeling (a type of mediumship), automatism, and psychic investigations. While some of these approaches can be used by laypeople to learn more about a ghost, an attempt to contact spirits should not be taken lightly. Not all ghosts are pleasant, and not all take kindly to having their eternity disturbed by curiosity seekers.

If at all possible, call on an expert to contact the ghost. If you can't get an expert, please take sensible precautions. Learn as much as possible about the system you choose for contacting the ghost. Heed any cautions and protective measures that you find during research, and remember to incorporate meaningful safeguards from your own beliefs.

When you ask to hear from the great beyond, request that only beneficent spirits attend your query. This is not perfectly foolproof, but it helps. Keep your questions respectful and brief, and never make the spirit tarry any longer than necessary. Always remain aware that no ghost or spirit has any right to infringe on your space, or to stay without your express permission. If you suddenly feel that the contacted entity is overstepping its boundaries, banish it firmly and close the spiritual door you opened—put that system away.

Automatism

Glossolalia, pendulum divination, and dowsing are all forms of the ancient practice of automatism. Automatism resembles mediumship, to the extent that it relies on an altered state of awareness. While in that state, the automatist is controlled by the spirit in question, which conveys information. Automatism comes spontaneously to some people, while others learn it as a skill.

Automatic Writing or Painting

Automatic writing, painting, and composition have given birth to numerous works of beauty. In the early 1900s, Pearl Curran wrote hundreds of acclaimed poems and stories, totaling more than 1,600,000 words, in a five-year period. She claimed to be channeling the spirit of Patience Worth, who helped her write *The Sorry Tale*. This was a story about one of Christ's contemporaries, which was remarkably accurate historically, given that it was written by an author with little education.

Creative artists in many fields rely on automatism. Matthew Manning and Luiz Gasparetto both attribute their painting abilities to spirit guidance. Gasparetto appeared on British television, producing an amazing 21 pictures in 75 minutes, with the help of his spirit. Rosemary Brown, who had very limited musical training, channeled music from famous composers. Her work was good enough to impress Leonard Bernstein.

Some researchers claim that automatism is merely a way to tap hidden or repressed skills or insights. Perhaps the manifestation of creative talent could be a form of ESP, whereby the automatist accesses the consciousness of other living people. But for those who believe in ghosts and the afterlife, automatism is one way to download information from the spiritual computer matrix that contains all human experience and memory. Ghosts seem to be able to tell their stories or express ideas through the artist's paintbrush or the composer's pen, as well as through the written word.

Ouija

The Ouija board originated in Asia Minor. The prototype consisted of a three-legged bronze table engraved with images of Hecate, a circular dish with sacred symbols, which functioned like a roulette wheel, and two rings. This apparatus was used to gather information from the next world. In 371 A.D., a more modernized version of the Ouija appeared in Greece. This consisted of a laurel tripod, a round metal plate inscribed with Greek letters, linen thread, and a suspended ring that acted like the modern planchette. The diviner set the ring in motion to begin the divination. Apart from this moment, the implement was never touched by mortal hands. The diviner invoked the spirits, trusting them to guide the tool to give correct answers. The Roman Emperor Valens used this early form of the Ouija to discover the name of his successor.

During the Victorian era, Ouija sessions were often conducted at mid-day teas. The popular interest in this system prompted the Psychical Research Society to conduct studies on the Ouija. In 1914, William Barrett, a representative of the Society, reported the belief that the Ouija exhibited "super-normal" results that could be attributed to noncorporeal spirits.

The Ouija has helped shaped modern metaphysical thought. Jane Roberts used it in 1973 to contact the entity known as Seth, whom she later channeled directly. Her "Seth" books were foundational documents for the popular interest in channeling spirits, which still continues.

The modern Ouija consists of a pointer called a "planchette," which glides over a board labeled with the letters of the alphabet, the words "yes" and "no," and sometimes the phrase "good-bye." Enquirers wishing to contact and question a spirit place their fingers lightly on the planchette and voice their question. At this moment, if a spirit has been contacted, the planchette will begin to move—seemingly on its own. The planchette stops to indicate individual letters, in a sequence that spells out the spirit's response.

The "game" that developed from this serious method of spiritual communication has tainted the reputation of Ouija. The game lacks safeguards: because of this, it is not a good system for determining ghostly presences and their stories. People who use Ouija as a game can never be wholly certain whether they have contacted the desired entity, contacted some other entity, or simply received information manipulated by the person using the planchette.

So, I mention Ouija here only with strong cautions attached. Always begin a Ouija session with some type of protective prayer or meditation. One prevalent visualization entails imagining yourself, the room, and everything within it, enveloped in white light. White is the color of purity and goodness. Work the board only with trusted friends; never use another person's family heirloom board; and *never* use it as a toy for amusement. This is a key for opening spiritual doors. What walks through that door can be unpleasant if there are no controls set in place, such as ritually created sacred space.

If no Ouija board is available, you can create one by laying out the letters of the alphabet in washable marker on erasable board. Make space for the words "yes" and "no." In the center, place an inverted glass: its mouth should be so small that it can only cover individual letters. Participants rest one or two fingertips on the base of the upside-down glass, and allow it to glide over the board.

If you contact a spirit, ask simple, direct questions. Questions that can be answered with a "yes" or "no" are best, because they don't tax the spirit's energy much. Should you, at any time during the inquiry, begin getting negative, malevolent messages from the board, stop all communications immediately and don't try this again. Angry, spiteful, or diabolic spirits only aid mortals when it serves their purposes. Moreover, if a spirit you have contacted begins making requests of you, do not honor these unless you deem them *reasonable* and plausible considering what you know of the spirit's predicament. Spirits, like people, can have their own agendas—which may not be in your best interest.

Channeling and Mediumship

Mediumship, recently called "channeling," has a rich history. In the biblical book of *Samuel*, Saul consults a medium—the Witch of Endor, who summons a spirit that answers Saul's questions. In pre-Buddhist Japan, inspired mediums were called upon to ask questions of supernatural beings. These questions and their answers decided important matters for entire communities. In later years, mediumship was a job for women, whose training helped draw the knowledgeable entity. Questions were posed, and the spirit was quickly dispatched back to its realm.

At the site of the Oracle of Delphi in classical Greece a woman known as the Pythia sat in the center of a shrine on a three-legged seat. Once the Pythia achieved a trance state, her words were regarded as coming from Apollo himself. So highly regarded were her skills that she was able to charge the ancient equivalent of millions of dollars for a single visit.

In Norse tradition, the prophetess was called Velda, Spakona ('woman of prophesy') or Volva ('seeress'). During the rite of mediumship, the Velda sat on an elevated seat, called *seiohjallr*, similar to the Delphic seat. Around it, singers chanted the required spells for augury. The Norse believed that singing and chanting attracted the spirits, who would then be consulted for their insight.

As with all metaphysical procedures, mediumship's popularity waxes and wanes according to the public's acceptance of mystical belief systems. At the turn of this century, mediumship was extraordinarily popular. This popularity came in the wake of the Spiritualist church, which used mediumship as its main method for communing with spirits. This form of spirit contact remains popular.

In a 1990 Gallup Poll, eleven percent of American adults indicated that they believed channeling had some validity. Studies conducted on channelers revealed an increase of alpha and beta waves, which differed from the patterns characteristic of a normal waking state, meditative state, and hypnotized state. What happens during the channeling session alters the medium's mind, according to these studies.

Most mediums follow the same basic procedures. First, the medium settles into a meditative state. A trance is entered, in which the medium's spirit leaves the body, or steps aside temporarily to make room for another entity. The medium then becomes a sort of astral radio receiver, translating and transmitting messages directly from the channeled entity to the querent.

There are two types of channeling—direct and ancillary: both forms of this ancient art have enjoyed a recent resurgence. Ruth Montgomery, author of *Herald of the New Age*, began contacting spirit guides in the 1960s. Her channeled information included hints of world change, which were incorporated into the New Age movement. Jack Pursel (who channels Lazarus) and J. Z. Knight (who channels Ramtha) are also well-known contemporary direct channelers.

In both direct channeling and ancillary channeling living people bring their questions to a sensitive, who is able to contact and communicate with the spirit world. Direct channelers, however, are voluntarily possessed by the spirit; ancillary channelers are not. In direct channeling, the spirit speaks directly to the querent; in ancillary channeling, the channeler listens to the spirit and recounts its answers to the querent

Ancillary channeling has its advantages. The psychic never relinquishes control of his or her body. The psychic may dismiss a spirit immediately, without needing to reverse a trance, if it appears to be an erroneous or negative contact. Last but not least, the psychic remains responsible for the messages he or she conveys.

A woman approached me one evening, saying she felt totally drained and depressed and had no idea why. She asked if I could contact her guides for insights into ways to alleviate, or at least diminish, this problem. I agreed, because I had known this woman for a while and could not remember ever seeing her so burdened. It was as if the weight of the world rested on her shoulders alone.

I began with a brief prayerful meditation to put myself in the right frame of mind, and then called upon her guides for aid. Oddly, they did not "appear" with a message. Instead, I felt their presence, and received a textural response. This was very unusual: no words came at all, only feeling.

Very confused, I shared this unique message with her. I explained first that I didn't understand the lack of words, but the message was quite clear. I had the distinct feeling of rich soil moving through my fingertips, followed by joyful emotions.

As I finished this wary statement, I looked up to see the woman crying. What had I done? I asked if anything was wrong, but found to my amazement that everything was "right." Apparently the woman had been considering a move to the country for the past year, but was afraid to lose the security of her job in the city. This struggle had unconsciously left her depressed and feeling unfulfilled. She left that night, resolving to achieve her goal, and did exactly that. She is now quite happy and successful, running a small farm in the country.

It is important to relay channeled information exactly as it comes. If I had not overcome my insecurity about the message, the woman might have left without hope, and without an answer. In this case, her observant spirit guides were more aware of her real needs than she was, and helped bring those needs to the forefront. This is an excellent example of how ancillary channeling can be an effective form of counseling, as well as a way to speak with ghosts.

At séances, the channeling can be either direct or ancillary. Several people—called "sitters"—gather to contact a specific spirit. The sitters hold hands around a table—this is called "forming a chain." The medium enters an altered state, often using a prayer or hymn and deep breathing to do so. While in that state, the medium can contact the spirit, and allow it to communicate. Mental mediums might see or hear the dead person (as in ancillary channeling), or might allow the spirit to possess them, partially (as in automatism) or wholly (as in direct channeling). Physical mediums work differently. When they contact a spirit, they produce environmental results such as materialization, temperature changes, or winds.

Critics of channeling and mediumship claim that much of the séance experience is either faked, or a result of subconscious prompting. A medium who knows human nature well can learn a lot from a querent's body language and from other subtle hints. Another theory is that mediumship is a type of ESP, in which the reader obtains nonverbal information from the querent, but attributes it to a spiritual source.

I believe that channeling and mediumship are skills anyone can acquire if he so chooses, but are not skills everyone *should* learn. People who have trouble focusing on single tasks, who are easily distracted or influenced, or who have trouble separating their personal opinions from presented materials, should probably not attempt to learn this art. Focus, clarity, and unbiased relaying of information are essential to an effective, safe channeling session.

Dream Work

Dreams have been considered a gift from spirits in other realms, or from the Divine. As we saw earlier in this book, they have a close connection to both sleep and death, and afford connection to the world of spirits. When people encounter a ghost in a dream, it is usually a loved one or friend, bringing a message to the living. Sometimes the message consoles and comforts, sometimes it contains advice or insights, and sometimes it is prophetic. Most people do not find these experiences alarming or frightening, but they do wake up startled by how real the dream visitation seemed. The dead usually initiate this form of contact. The open-minded state of the sleeper makes this a good opportunity for a ghost to communicate.

It is more difficult for the living to initiate dream contact with the dead. However, some people can initiate a rapport with the dead during sleep. They set up a protected space before retiring, meditating deeply on the person they wish to contact, and allowing that meditation to urge them gently into sleep. Sometimes personal objects that belonged to the deceased are kept near the bed to help draw the spirit's energy near.

Unless you feel confident about your ability to separate the dream world from the waking world, and can also control your dreams, I don't recommend you attempt this alone. Instead, ask a friend to sit with you through the night. Then, if you have a negative experience and need to shake it off, someone is there to provide assistance and comfort.

Skeptical Advisor: Many psychologists believe that the mind creates a story while we sleep, building pictures around symbols. Some of these symbols come from everyday life; others originate in the subconscious. According to this view, if a person seems to receive "communications" from the dead while dreaming, his mind is in fact resolving subconscious feelings toward, and issues with, the deceased.

Sensitives and Psychics

The word "psychic" comes from "psyche," meaning mind or soul. Psychics and sensitives are highly attuned to and aware of ever-present energies that remain undetectable by most folk. An effective sensitive picks up vibrations, past or present, that are in or around a site or object. He or she must then determine which vibrations are connected to ghostly events.

You will rarely find a good psychic or sensitive in the yellow pages. Let word of mouth and personal recommendations guide you to one. If you choose to employ a psychic to help resolve a ghost's riddle, make sure you get references first, and check them thoroughly. Interview the prospective candidates, asking questions until you feel confident that one person can do the job properly. Make sure that the lines of trust and communication are open between you and the sensitive. Remember that this person, no matter how talented, may not succeed. Whether the sensitive's approach works depends on many variables, including everyday difficulties and disruptions. Don't expect a miracle worker, but do expect a helper.

> *Skeptical Advisor:* The skeptical advisor here councils you that some purported sensitives are not what they seem. Unless you know something your sensitive doesn't know about the ghost, you may be fooled by opportunists looking to make a quick buck. This is why I stress networking as the key to finding reliable psychics.

Appendices

"Let the mind be enlarged, according to its capacity, to the grandeur of the mysteries, and not the mysteries contracted to the narrowness of the mind."

—Sir Francis Bacon

Spirit Superstitions

"The Soul, Immortal as its Sire, shall never die."
—Robert Montgomery

Superstitions have given us one way to explain what seems inexplicable, and to protect ourselves from the ruthless whims of fate. Not surprisingly, there is an abundance of lore regarding death, ghosts, ghostly phenomena, and anything associated with the dead. This appendix provides you with a small sampling of this rich legacy. Most of these entries are presented purely for your enjoyment, but you may decide to adopt some of them in your own efforts to contact ghosts, put a spirit to rest, or protect yourself from wandering souls.

Animal Omens

- In England, a large black snail appearing on the doorstep of a home may be the spirit of a deceased family member.

- In Scotland, a storm petrel indicates someone will die soon; it may also be the spirit of a sailor who died at sea.

- In certain African tribal societies, a white bird flying into a prayer hut bears the spirit of an ancestor who brings blessings.

- The cry of an owl presages death. Where it builds a nest, ghosts will haunt for as long as the bird stays.

(The crowing of a cock signals wandering ghosts that it is time for them to disappear until nightfall.

(Both horses and dogs can sense the presence of spirits.

Binding a Ghost or Spirit

(Tie seven, fourteen, or twenty-one knots into a rope, while naming the soul you wish to restrict. Bury this outside the home to keep that spirit out, or burn the rope to release the spirit to another existence.

(In Malaysia, sacred water combined with incense is said to expel the grasshopper demon.

(Pinching a possessed person and blowing on his or her head banishes the unwanted spirit and returns the human spirit to its body. This tradition also comes from Malaysia.

(If someone is possessed with the spirit of sickness, have him or her drink coconut juice, followed by a bland diet for at least one week. This person should try to maintain emotional and digestive balance from that time forward to keep the malevolent spirit away.

(In the sixteenth century, a common recipe for banishing unwanted spirits was to fast, pray, drink wine mixed with holy oil, and carry appropriate religious charms or relics.

(Scatter dill mixed with salt, fennel, and mullein all around the area in which the ghost or spirit is believed to reside.

(Burning frankincense and myrrh may not completely banish spirits, but it helps give them peace and rest.

(Hang a garlic wreath over your doorway. Whenever a spirit plagues you, bite a piece—then toss it away from the house. This carries the spirit with it.

(Gather knot grass by the waning moon. Take this to the area where the ghost abides and tie one knot in it. Bury this to confine the spirit to the grave.

(Burying a person's shadow in a specific location prior to his or her death will prevent the spirit from leaving that spot.

(In Denmark, there is a tradition that you can pin a ghost to a location using a wooden post. If the post is pulled up, however, the ghost will be freed.

Preventing Ghosts

(Closing the eyes of the dead before burial keeps their spirits from wandering.

(In Greece, dancing around the burial site of an enemy was a way to keep that person's spirit from returning for revenge.

(Wash the threshold of your house immediately after a dead body is removed. This keeps the spirit of that person from returning.

(Within the burial site, always place a cross of iron. This will keep the spirit of that person in the grave.

(Egyptians wrapped their mummies in sweet spices so the soul smelled pleasant to the guardians of the next world, who would then allow the soul to enter its new existence.

(Provide the body with things that it loved in life—a few coins, some good wine, and so on. This brings contentment to the spirit.

(In Spain, to guarantee that the soul rests peacefully, people at the wake danced seven times around the body. Prayers were recited for the same purpose.

(In India, placing a sprig of basil in the coffin provided the spirit with a peaceful journey.

(If the clothing of the dead contains any knots this will keep the spirit from moving on. Untie these before burial.

(Open all the doors and windows in the area where the person died so the spirit can have quick passage.

(When someone is deathly ill keep all the animals out of the house so the person's spirit will not possess him.

(Before burial, place pennies on the eyes of the dead, tie their toes together so they cannot walk, and put open scissors—forming a cross—on their chest.

(Never cry at funerals. Tears falling on the dead make it more difficult for the spirit to disengage and leave this world.

(Bury the body at a border or near a crossroad. These places are considered a type of limbo that no spirit can leave.

(After burial, plant thorn bushes around both the grave and your home. The spirit will get tangled in them, and be unable to pass back into the house.

(If a person did not receive a proper burial or cremation, give him or her one. This will stop a haunting.

Protection from the Dead

(Lodestone is a protective talisman against spirits. This may be due to its association with iron.

(Plant houseleeks on your roof. The Latin name for this plant, *sempervivium*, means "ever living," and the dead cannot bear its presence.

(Cover all your mirrors immediately after a death. This keeps a spirit from using them as a portal.

(Jump into running water, or cross it. A spirit cannot follow you there: moving water represents life.

(The Aztecs considered jimson weed a sacred plant that would protect from ghosts any area in which it grew.

(Bonfires and other light sources drive away malevolent spirits, like those that walk the earth more freely on Midsummer, Hallows, and Lammas, so it was traditional to build fires then. In the Middle Ages, people left candles near their beds to drive away spirits. On Hallows specifically, people carried turnips with candles inside—the original of the Jack-o-Lantern—for protection.

(Place a sprig of rosemary inside a seashell. Bind it within, using a red thread. Carry this with you as an amulet against ghosts.

(Hang rowan and St. John's Wort over the doorway of your home, and no malicious spirits can enter therein.

(Write the letters AGLA in the center of a hexagram and carry this token with you. The hexagram repels evil spirits and misfortune. Cabalists used this formula to banish spirits.

(Angelica and nettle worn or carried as an amulet will protect the bearer from evil spirits.

(Sleeping on the skin of an ass and drinking boneset tea keeps away devilish ghosts.

(Bathing in fennel water, or drinking it, protects one against the spirit of disease.

(In Greece, growing violets in or around a home was considered an effective ward against wandering spirits.

(If you are being chased by a ghost, pass through the cleft of a tree. This confuses the spirit, and you will be safe.

Seeing or Attracting Ghosts

(A child born at midnight, known as a chime child, has the gift of sight, as does the seventh son of a seventh son.

- Mayas of the Yucatan draw a chalk line from the grave to the hearth of the deceased's home. The spirit can then find its way back to visit, whenever it wishes.

- If you know a spirit's true name, you can evoke it.

- Ghosts are more readily seen and contacted at midnight (the time in between day and night), and on the anniversary of their death.

- The veil between worlds grows thin, and ghostly activity increases, during New Year's celebrations, and on festivals for the dead—Halloween is both.

- Medieval spell books say that burning a mixture of aloe, musk, saffron, vervain, and pepper in a cemetery will allow you to see the spirits that reside there.

- In the Middle Ages, some felt that washing a clean piece of steel in mugwort juice would summon a spirit.

- Belladonna fumes—CAUTION! These are poisonous!—were often included in incense for invoking spirits and ghosts.

- Children born on Christmas will be specially blessed: they will never see a dreaded spirit.

- Write the name of the spirit you wish to invoke on parchment, and burn it while repeating sacred words to help draw that spirit to you.

Signs of Impending Death
- A clock that stops inexplicably.

(A clock that chimes randomly between the hours.

(The presence of a "winding sheet" on a candle. This is a long sheet of wax, melting off one side of the candle and looking like a cloth. (Winding sheets have also been said to signify the presence of a ghost.)

(Bees swarming down the chimney.

(Birds flying into a house or banging against the windows.

(An owl hooting persistently, near the home.

(A lone raven flying over the house.

Historical Haunts

When you unravel the mysteries of your own ghosts, you may find that your interest in this topic has grown. If so, it might be fun, interesting, and enlightening to visit places known for their spiritual residents. Many of these sites are terrific landmarks or tourist attractions. This appendix lists some of these locations. A number of theses places have been haunted for hundreds of years. Some spiritualists believe that their long history indicates that they are gateways to the afterlife.

Ashley Restaurant

Rockledge, Florida

Built in the 1920s, this two-story restaurant houses an odd variety of disembodied patrons. A woman murdered there in the 1930s haunts the ladies' room, making disturbing sounds when it is otherwise vacant. Photographs reveal a specter wearing clothing from the late 1920s. Elsewhere in the restaurant, manifestations usually occur at night, or early in the morning. Glasses and dishes fly or break by themselves, whispers and buzzing are heard, and local police report alarms going off with no apparent cause.

Beckett's CastleCape

Elizabeth, Maine

Built in 1871, this home was originally owned and occupied by

Sylvester Beckett, a noted publisher and avid Spiritualist. Most locals believe Mr. Beckett haunts the house in order to prove Spiritualism's theory that life goes on after death. Mr. Beckett likes to force open doors (even those that have been secured shut), and to rearrange artwork that displeases him.

Bisham Abbey
Berkshire, England
In its glory days, this was the home of the Renaissance translator Thomas Hoby, and his wife, Dame Elizabeth. Dame Elizabeth haunts the halls, carrying a basin and washing her hands before disappearing. In life, the dame had little patience for ignorance or slovenliness. When one of her sons exhibited both, she beat him to death in a fit of rage, then swore the family to silence. Local legend has it that the boy's school supplies were later uncovered at the Abbey, bearing witness to his life and sad death.

Country House Restaurant
Clarendon Hills, Illinois
The shutters and doors of this two-story structure open and close of their own volition. The scent of lilacs fills the air, the jukebox goes on, the sounds of a woman weeping continue through the night, and slow footsteps often meticulously walk where no person stands. The story is that a young woman committed suicide just outside the restaurant in 1957, due to a lover's quarrel with the bartender. Her spirit has waited here for her love, ever since.

Dozmary Pool

Cornwall, England

In this location the spirit of Tregeagle carries out its bidden assignment. Tregeagle was a terribly dishonest and tyrannical judge, whose ghost haunted the general area until banished to the pool by a local priest. The priest gave the ghost a task: Tregeagle must empty the legendary bottomless well, using nothing more than a limpet shell.

Edgehill

Warwickshire, England

Edgehill was host to one of the main battles of the English Civil War. In 1642, 4,000 men died here. On the following Yule, and frequently thereafter, local shepherds and other witnesses reported seeing a full repetition of the battle—complete with drums, muskets, and standards. Even Charles I bore witness to this manifestation. The frequency of sightings has slowly decreased, indicating that this is an energy imprint that will fade with time.

Fata Morgana

Straits of Messina, Sicily

The mythical character of Morgana lends her name to a special type of "haunt," believed by some to be nothing more than an optical illusion. The Fata Morgana is a mirage-like image that appears in various parts of the world—including the Firth of Forth in Scotland and Mt. Fairweather, Alaska. One of the more detailed accounts of the spectacle came from a friar named Minasi, who lived in the late eighteenth century. While sailing, the good friar noticed an odd fog hovering above the waters. Suddenly all manner of arches, castles, columns, and towers extended themselves 20–30 feet above the foggy waters: armies, herds, and bountiful trees could be seen in this land-scape. The images disappeared as quickly and mysteriously as they came.

Fatima Apparition

Various Locations

The first Fatima apparitions began in 1917 and were seen by thou-sands of people over a six-month period. The vision was described by Lucia Santos—the first person to see it—as an angel of peace: it remained an unspoken secret until its reality was confirmed by re-peated visitations. One of the children involved in later encounters believed this was actually the spirit of Mary. The child invited every-one to return on the thirteenth of the month, when the spirit had promised to return. Many people who came reported unusual events, including glistening globules in the sky, a shining disk danc-ing overhead, humming sounds like that of a loud bee (in some myths a divine messenger), and a light-filled figure hovering over the ground. Some researchers might consider these reports congru-ent with modern UFO sightings.

Gilsland Castle

Cumberland, England

A small child was locked away on the highest floor of this keep, as punishment. When the temperature dropped, the boy froze to death. Since then his spirit walks the hall checking on slumbering guests. If a guest is gravely ill, the boy will touch the guest, saying "Forever cold you shall be." Inevitably, the ailing person dies soon thereafter.

Glamis Castle
Scotland

Within the large and stately manor of Glamis there is a secret room, known only to a few members of the Strathmore family. Folklore claims that one member of the family, terribly disfigured and quite mad, lived a miserable life locked within that room. To this day the ghost shrieks and struggles to free itself from captivity.

Other spirits frequent Glamis as well. One is an unknown, tongueless woman, who clutches at her mouth. Another woman—a white lady—floats in the hallways. A tiny page seems to be forever waiting to tend to his duties, and the Lord of the manor himself is always seen in his bedchamber, playing cards. It was here, say the bards, that he lost his soul to the devil in a card game. Louder than all these restless folk by far, however, are the ever-screaming spirits of the Ogilvy clan—a clan Lord Strathmore locked in the tower and left to die, in the seventeenth century.

Hermitage Castle
Scotland

This keep boasts of having the spirit of Lord Soulis as its eternal guest. Lord Soulis made a pact with the devil in order to obtain power on this earth. Accordingly, he lived in luxury and pleasure, but when death was imminent he confessed his sin to his servants. These good folk worried for the Lord's fate. When he died, they laid his body on a pyre to be consumed by flames, hoping to save his soul from hell. Alas, the spirit could not go to heaven either—so it remains in Hermitage, wandering the halls.

Holy Trinity Church
York, England
This sacred structure houses the spirit of a feisty, immutable nun. As local legend has it, during the Civil War a band of soldiers were intent on ransacking the holy structure. The abbess warned them they would be damned for their sacrilege, and proceeded to take up a sword and kill several of the invaders. Eventually, her valiant efforts failed—but her spirit remains behind to safeguard the church forever.

Island of Samsø
Scandinavia
A famous burial ground for Vikings who explored the northern seas, this island welcomes the restless dead as eternal guests. There are numerous reports of fires over the tombs at night. Some of these fires are spiritual guardians keeping robbers away from Viking treasures; others are the spirits of the Vikings themselves. Those souls brave enough to visit here say that the floating embers are not hot, but cold as death itself.

Killicrankie Pass
Scotland
At dawn, dusk, or midnight, come and stand at this pass: if there is

fog in the hills, all the better. From here you can see a spectral re-enactment of a battle from 1689, between Viscount Dundee and the English. According to witnesses' reports, this is a bloody battle, complete with hordes of Highlanders in kilts. The entire battle replays itself. After all the combatants have fallen, scavenger birds and treasure gatherers appear.

Liberty Hall Museum
Frankfort, Kentucky
Built in 1796 as the home of John Brown, one of the first Kentucky senators, this is now a tourist attraction. Locals tell the story of a gray lady who walks the gardens or looks out windows. Most believe this is the spirit of Margaret Varick, an aunt of Brown's who died of a heart attack while visiting here.

There is another ghost gracing these halls: a Spanish opera singer came for a party one night and went for a walk in the gardens, never to be heard from again—at least not in life. The third ghost of Liberty Hall is the spirit of a soldier from the 1800s. This spirit always comes to the windows of the museum at night, hoping for a glimpse of a lady whom he wished to court.

Marwell Hall
Hampshire, England
This simple English home is no longer haunted, but its story is well worth sharing. Here a young bride, intent on playing hide-and-seek with her groom and guests, disappeared. People searched the countryside for days, and only realized she was dead when her spirit began

to float along the hallways and try to open locks. Many years later, a servant discovered her resting place. In an attic, tucked neatly in an old oak chest, was a skeleton wearing a bridal gown. Once this was uncovered, the ghost never appeared again.

The Mount
Lenox, Massachusetts
This was the home of author Edith Wharton in the early 1900s. People hear constant footsteps in this old house, along with the faint sound of dresses touching a wooden floor. Over the years, Mrs. Wharton has been seen along with her lover and her husband.

Poe House
Baltimore, Maryland
A two-story home built in the 1830s, this was the home and work-place of Edgar Allan Poe, who took up residence in its attic for several years. During a period when the house was uninhabited, neighbors called the police after seeing lights move through the house into the attic. Police surrounded the building and waited for a tour guide to arrive with a key. No one was found. Tourists mention being tapped on the shoulder and hearing noises from the third floor. While no one is certain who the spiritual residents are, sightings of an elderly woman suggest that one ghost is Poe's aging aunt, who died in the house.

The Queen Mary
Port of Long Beach, California

This tourist attraction has 390 rooms to house the living or the dead. The Queen Mary made 1,001 Atlantic voyages while it sailed, and now many believe it to be haunted. Tour guides, former captains, paranormal experts, and guests have described unusual phenomena. These include hovering lights near the old morgue, sensor alarms going off in sealed regions, footsteps, rushes of air, and visual manifestations. Surprisingly, none of the spirits seem malevolent, even though their company includes a murdered cook and a drowned guest.

Ram Inn
Gloucestershire, England

The experiences of guests here range from cold spots (as one might anticipate in a drafty old inn) to reports of mist, disembodied voices, floating objects, electrical surges, and balls of light. Research revealed that the inn lies on ancient Norman foundations, above an even older Saxon ritual site.

Tower of London
London, England

Perhaps one of the most haunted places on earth, with a bloody history. At different times, the tower has served as a prison, a place of torture and execution, a barracks, and even a temporary royal residence. Numbers of restless ghosts frequent its halls.

The ghosts of Edward and Richard Plantagenet—who were

murdered in 1483 on the orders of their uncle—are silent guests, always seen walking together, hand in hand. The Countess of Salisbury was executed for treason in 1541. Her actual offense may have been that she was the mother of Cardinal Pole, who vehemently opposed Henry VIII's break with the Church of Rome. The Countess appears in the courtyard, running wildly from her executioner, until he succeeds at his duty.

The graceful Lady Jane Grey appears on each anniversary of her 1554 execution. Sir Walter Raleigh, who had the questionable distinction of being incarcerated here for thirteen years before being beheaded, is another ghostly presence. The ghost of Anne Boleyn, the unfortunate second wife of Henry the VIII, appears without a head. Anne was beheaded in 1536 for adultery, and her spirit seems still to defy Henry.

Versailles Palace

Versailles, France

Built in the seventeenth century, the palace houses the spirit of Marie Antoinette, who met her fate on the guillotine in 1793. It also contains imprints of servants, buildings, gardens, and walkways that vanished long ago. The best time to see these manifestations is near dusk, when shadows of the past seep through into our reality.

Virgin Mary Sightings

Various Locations

The spirit of Mary is an enduring visitation, with reports of group sightings noted as recently as the 1980s. In Lourdes, France, witnesses in 1858 reported odd lights, a dancing sun, buzzing sounds, and silent communications exhorting repentance of sin. Other sites have similar histories. For those wishing to experience this, Italy is a good place to visit. It seems to be Mary's favorite country in the world, producing approximately 35 percent of the reported apparitions.

Two other regions worth exploring are Medjugorje in Bosnia and Zeitoun in Egypt. Sightings in Medjugorje began in 1981 and were investigated by Henri Joyeux. Joyeux reported that the participants were not dreaming, because their eye movements seemed synchronized—indicating some type of common visual input. Zeitoun, Egypt, is, according to legend, the place where Mary and Joseph rested during their flight from Herod. Visitations here began in 1968 and stopped in 1971. They were experienced by about 200,000 people. The common reports in this region mentioned luminous phenomena hovering above the Church of Mary, some of which were photographed.

See also: Fatima Apparitions.

White Bull Alley

Lancashire, England

This small walkway is one that animals refuse to tread willingly. Stories claim that it is inhabited by the lone figure of a woman who walks silently by night, carrying her basket. If you talk to her, she will begin to laugh hideously; more precisely, her basket laughs—it contains her head, long since separated from her body. The head, which seems to have much life still left in it, jumps from the basket to taunt the unsuspecting. While no one knows who this woman was, her fate in life seems clear, as does her ire. To this day, local children do not venture into the alley even in daylight, for fear of her presence.

Winchester House
San Jose, California

Sara Winchester, heiress to the Winchester Rifle Company's fortune, believed deeply in ghosts. When a medium told her that the spirits of those killed by Winchester rifles wished her ill, she built a home where any spirit would be happy to dwell. Construction began in 1884, and the completed building had 160 rooms and thirteen baths. The thirteenth bathroom sported thirteen windows. The séance room had thirteen coat hooks for guests. In 1923, the Winchester house became a tourist attraction, which people believe is inhabited by Sara's ghost, and by the spirits she welcomed in its creation. Guests and staff continue to report whispers, opening and closing doors, music, dancing lights, and cold spots throughout the house.

Witch Hollow Farm
Boxford, Massachusetts

Built in 1666, this farm is the eternal haunt of Mary Tyler, a young woman found guilty of witchcraft at Salem in 1693. Mary lived in this home as a child, and apparently returned to the site of happier days upon her death. Manifestations here include visual sightings by moonlight, rustling noises, whispering, an odd floating green light, and banging in the attic, predominantly at night.

Woodbon House (now the Governor's Mansion)

Dover, Delaware

Originally constructed in 1790, this mansion housed many families and is reputed to have four ghosts. One is a thirsty spirit—it will drink any wine left unattended! An elderly colonel from the Revolutionary War haunts this mansion, as does a little girl in gingham skirts. An unsavory fellow, a slave kidnapper in life, spends the nights rattling chains.

A Lexicon of the Afterlife

adjuration A formula for the purpose of exorcism, an adjuration uses sacred words or phrases to command a spirit. From the Latin phrase *ad jurare*, meaning "to swear to."

ancillary channeling A spiritual ability in which a channeler calls a spirit to himself or herself, listens to that spirit, and conveys the spirit's information. The spirit does not possess the ancillary channeler.

angel Sometimes mistaken for a ghost, an angel is a divine, protective messenger. It often appears surrounded by light, or formed out of light. The Greek word *angelos* means "messenger."

anima mundi The vital soul of the earth that is connected to the universe; its energy is reflected in all of nature. This concept was originally proposed by the Stoic philosophers of ancient Greece, and later reinforced by sacred geometry.

Ankou In Brittany, the spirit of Cain's son, doomed to roam the earth, forever collecting souls. In early European history, people left offerings to Ankou on their threshold to appease death and keep it away.

apparition A supernatural occurrence, such as a ghost sighting, that cannot be explained as a natural occurrence. Apparitions of humans, animals, vehicles, and various objects have been seen. The Titanic's ghostly image is a notable example.

Apsares Ghosts of noble Hindu warriors who haunt rivers and pools, functioning somewhat like the water nymphs of European lore.

astral body Formed of energy or light, the astral body contains the feelings and experiences of the individual. Astral bodies separate from the physical body, and can be seen by others during Out-of-Body Experiences (OBEs) and Near-Death Experiences (NDEs).

aura The luminous sphere of energy that surrounds living things, auras are also depicted as haloes on the saints, in many traditions of painting. The sixteenth-century occultist Paracelsus described the appearance of the aura as a fiery glove. Modern writings state that this field shifts in size, color, and intensity according to the being's moods, health, and mental activity. Some people therefore believe that the spirit manifests externally as an aura.

automatism The ability to allow information to flow effortlessly from a spirit to a living being, as in **channeling**, **mediumship**, and automatic writing. Pendulum divination, Ouija boards, and table-tipping are also considered automatism.

autoscopy A phenomenon reported by those who have experienced **OBEs** and **NDEs**. In autoscopy one sees a visual image of one's own body from outside.

ba Egyptian term for the human soul. The ba left the body after death, but was destined to return to the body eventually. Artists depicted it as looking much like an **angel**—as a winged human form that rested in the stars until its return to earth.

banshee In Scotland and Ireland, this spirit appears prior to a person's death, keening to mourn the family's loss, and to welcome him or her into the afterlife.

bardo A Tibetan term that refers to an intermediate state. The so-called "Tibetan Book of the Dead" describes three bardos that may be undergone by a dying or dead person. This book is read aloud by a Lama to a dying person, and for forty-nine days after death, in order to help the person avoid confusion during the transition and attain liberation.

bilocation The phenomenon of someone appearing to be in two places at one time. Only one of those images is truly physical. Two Christian saints—St. Anthony and St. Ambrose—were reputed to have this ability, which is known today as a willed **OBE**.

boggle Northern English term for a poltergeist or mischievous sprite.

boogie man The childhood "monster" ghost, who is supposed to live under the bed, or in the closet.

bourru In Persia, a ghost that looked like an old monk walking the streets around midnight.

bridge of sands Once over this bridge, the spirit cannot return to its body, but passes into its next existence. It appears in Greek, English, Chinese, and Norse myth. Consequently, a **ghost** is a spirit that neither crossed this bridge, nor returned to its body.

cabalist A Hebrew mystic.

Cacodaemon A Greek word for a malevolent spirit that tries to possess humans for evil purposes. By extension, Cacodemonomania refers to a mental disorder caused by a bad spirit.

cemetery light Bluish lights seen after dark hovering, then disappearing, near burial grounds, especially freshly dug sites.

chain, forming a At the beginning of a **séance**, participants join hands in a circle to create a protected area. To maintain this safe zone, the chain should not be broken at any time during a séance.

channeling Channelers and **mediums** transmit messages from spirits in the astral realm. They become a sort of inter-dimensional telephone line.

clairaudience The ability to hear clearly the voices of **ghosts**, and other sounds normally inaudible to the human ear.

clairvoyance The ability to "see" in the mind's eye residual memories from an object or place and to describe them.

Cloud People Pueblo spirits with whom the spirits of the dead—the Ancestors—are identified. The Cloud People live in the four corners of creation.

conjure To summon or urge a spirit to manifest itself, usually for a specific task such as answering questions.

corpse candle An odd light that presages death, considered to be a type of **Will-o'-the-Wisp**.

deathbed vision Unlike the **Near-Death Experience**, a deathbed vision is described as it occurs. Most are positive and last about five minutes, during which time the person sees relatives and a bright light, and experiences an overall feeling of welcome.

death coach An English spirit that collects souls. If one sees this phenomenon, a death is occurring, or has very recently taken place.

demon The evil spirit of a fallen **angel** in Christian tradition.

devas Semi-divine entities that are intimately connected with nature, specifically the four elements. In European tradition, the water devas are undines, the earth devas are gnomes or dwarves, air devas are sylphs or **fairies**, and fire devas are salamanders. The belief in devas appears in other cultures as well, including those of ancient Persia and Tibet.

disincarnate Of a form that exists outside the physical body.

doppelganger German word for the body's double, which appears just before, or at the time of, a person's death. The English poet Percy Bysshe Shelley reported sighting such a creature shortly before he drowned.

dowsing A type of divination that uses a forked rod to determine the location of something. A spiritual presence can be located by this method.

duppy In Jamaica, there is a belief that people have two souls—one good, one evil. On the third day after death, the good soul may return to Africa, while the other becomes a duppy—a spirit that hovers in various forms near the grave. Duppies are traditionally most active at noon and midnight, when it is best not to be standing at crossroads or in doorways.

dybbuk, or dibbuk Some Eastern European Jewish traditions describe this entity as the wandering spirit of a dead person who seeks to possess bodies. The dybbuk goes from one body to the next, in order to have a vehicle in which to atone for earthly failures and faults.

earth sound A noise heard in rural areas that seems to have no origin and is often mistaken for a **poltergeist** or other ghostly manifestation. People describe these sounds as varying from a low throb to loud, shaking bursts. Earth sounds may have geological origins.

ectoplasm A whitish emission of light near a medium ectoplasm forms itself into shapes, to confirm a spiritual presence. Most reports of ectoplasm have been debunked. Nonetheless, it is interesting that many ghostly apparitions bear a whitish, semi-formed quality.

Electronic Visual or Voice Phenomena (EVP) Purported spiritual manifestations appearing in TV or radio static, EVP resemble the form, or convey the speech, of a known dead person.

Extra-Sensory Perception (ESP) ESP allows a person's mind to gather knowledge or information, without using normal sensory input. Forms of ESP include telepathic experiences, **clairvoyance**, paranormal awareness, and precognition. ESP, according to studies from the last 40 years, is more likely to occur when a person is inactive and alone, away from external distractions. More than 49 percent of Americans believe in some form of ESP.

fairy A **deva** whose pranks are sometimes mistaken for the activities of a **ghost** or **poltergeist**. Numerous types of fairies are believed to exist, each of which is connected to an element. Gnomes, for example, are earth fairies. Undines are water fairies. Sylphs inhabit the air, and salamanders embody fire.

fetch Old English term for a spiritual body double, likely caused by an **Out-of-Body Experience** or **Near-Death Experience**. See **doppelganger**.

fetters Objects, places, or people that bind a spirit to this world.

floaters Cells that leak into the vitreous liquid of the eye and can be seen as small circles in one's field of vision. Floaters are physical, but they are sometimes mistaken for psychic energy or spirits.

fox fire The glow seen on rotting logs or stumps in the dark, emitted by certain types of fungus. Some scientists suggest this may be one cause for phenomena such as **Will-o'-the-Wisp** and **ghost lights**.

fylgja A Scandinavian spirit double that may take the form of any human or animal. In an Icelandic saga, the hero Njal goes into the battlefield with the god Thor and sees a bloodied fylgja just before his death. In some regions the fylgja is considered an attendant, guardian, and guide in this life and the next. It comes to earth when a child is born and stays with that person throughout life.

Ga-Oh Seneca Indian spirit that controls and lives in the winds.

ghost An apparition, often shadowy, of a dead person. The word comes from the Anglo-Saxon *gaest*—a shadow or trace of breath or spirit, or a faint secondary image. Researchers reserve this term for recurrent **apparitions** of spirits believed trapped between the worlds. Most ghost sightings are visual. One third of sightings are also auditory. Most ghosts seem dimly aware of the living beings who see them.

ghost light Generally seen as bobbing and circular luminescence, ghost lights last up to fifteen minutes. The largest number of these luminescent phenomena occur in the mountains of North Carolina. In the Andes, a ghost light sighting portends success in finding hidden treasures. There have been reports of ghost lights on the water off New Brunswick, where the sea often seems to glow prior to storms. These ghost lights change into light-filled columns. See **St. Elmo's Fire.**

glaisrig In Scottish tradition, a water-dwelling spirit that protects young children and the elderly.

glossolalia Speaking in tongues.

gremlin An impish, mischievous being of the air, of small stature and great strength.

harpies Spirits in Greek mythology that caused tempests and tried to steal food. Known as ravagers, harpies are described as having the body and claws of a bird, the face of a hog, and the ears of a bear.

haunting From an old English word meaning "to fetch home." Hauntings, or recurring ghostly visitations at a specific location, have been reported by every culture in every historical context. Such visitations are not necessarily made by **ghosts** of humans. Hauntings include repeated sightings of animal spirits and self-propelled objects, like a candlestick floating in air. Signs of a haunt include mysterious sounds, drafts, temperature changes, objects moving of their own accord, and unusual light manifestations.

hexagram A geometric form used as a protective sigil.

invisible presence A feeling that one is not alone, often engendered by quiet and darkness.

jiva Jain word for the life principle within all things. This energy is indestructible and unquantifiable.

Ka Egyptian version of the **fetch** or **doppelganger**.

kbotermannekens In Flemish lore, these spirits love to trick female dairy workers. At times, people mistake them for **ghosts** or sprites.

kelpie A spiteful spirit, one of which inhabits every stream, pond, and lake in Scotland.

khmoc pray An evil Cambodian tree spirit that forms when a person experiences a violent or early death.

kirkenauer Scandinavian term for the wandering spirit of a sacrificed animal that visits church yards or pews at night.

kliwa A fearsome, airborne spirit in Taos culture. Its breath bears all manner of sickness.

luminous body A faint glow in a dead body that signifies a soul's imminent departure.

medium A person who communicates with spirits, often during trance states. There are two types of mediumship—physical and mental. Physical mediumship manifests in the medium's behavior and in the environment through phenomena such as rapping and breezes. The mental medium hears and sees spirits and can communicate information from them. At times, the mental medium may voluntarily allow spirit possession to channel more information.

memory imprint An energy remnant that leaves a mark on a room or region. Memory imprints act like a psychic photograph or repeated movie loop, and can be discerned by some people.

mountaintop glow Blazing sheets of light that appear on the Andean peaks of Bolivia, Peru, and Chile, and also seen in some regions of the Alps. Researchers consider this a type of **St. Elmo's Fire**, but many natives attribute these mysterious phenomena to ancestors or gods.

Navky In Slavic cultures, the ghost of an unbaptized child or the spirit of a child killed by its mother. The Navky wails and cries in trees, sometimes distracting travelers or asking strangers for aid as they pass.

Near-Death Experiences (NDEs) A group of phenomena recounted by people who have been briefly dead, or have come very close to death. The Egyptian *Book of the Dead* alludes to NDEs and explains what the newly deceased can expect to encounter. Accounts of NDEs are not limited to any particular religious or social group, and all survivors of such experiences say it changes their perception of death dramatically. The study of NDEs has contributed supporting evidence that ghosts and some form of afterlife are possible.

necromancy A type of divination in which the diviner or necromancer contacts one or more spirits of the dead, to obtain information. In some instances the spirit is conjured to appear; in others—such as Ouija sessions—it communicates less directly.

numinous experience The feeling of being in the presence of a supernatural power, force, or entity. Sweeping emotions like awe, ecstasy, humility, or confusion may follow. Generally, this is an encounter with a Master-Teacher or a divine entity, rather than a ghostly encounter.

ocean lights A phenomenon in which a body of water seems to radiate with bands or wheels of light, seen especially in the Indian Ocean and south China Sea during August and January. Sailors and natives to these regions attribute such sightings to spirits.

Ouija board A flat board, printed with letters and the words "yes" and "no." The Ouija board is used in conjunction with a pointer, to ask questions of spirits.

Out-of-Body Experiences (OBEs) Similar to **NDEs**, but the person having the experience is not in danger of dying. Surveys estimate that eight to fifteen percent of the population has experienced some form of OBE. Many cultures were interested in this phenomenon, and have credited their holy persons with willed OBEs. Enoch, in the Old Testament, is one example. During OBEs, people remain aware of their physical and astral bodies as well as their surroundings, their senses seem heightened, and they feel more liberated.

paranormal Of an occurrence that extends beyond the boundary of rational cause and effect. The word means "beside the normal."

parapsychology The peripheral areas of psychology in which the cause and effect of paranormal experiences are studied. Generally, this field focuses on testing **extra-sensory perception** and psychokinesis in controlled settings. Max Dessoir, a German psychical researcher, coined the term.

pendulum divination A form of divination using an object suspended by string over a region. The movements of the object determine the answers to questions; sometimes the questions are posed to spirits.

planchette An early version of the **Ouija** board, this tool was created to reach the world of spirits. Made from wood shaped like a heart, and placed on casters, it is fitted with a pencil. In one type of **automatism**, a **medium** places his or her hand on the planchette, which then writes a message. The pointer that glides over a modern Ouija board is stilled called a planchette.

poltergeist A spiritual entity that tends toward noisy and sometimes violent outbursts. Reports of poltergeists survive from first century Rome, and were common in the Middle Ages and Renaissance. They were even reported by Martin Luther. More recent studies indicate that poltergeist activity usually lasts from two weeks to two months, with some manifestations extending for more than a year. The activity centers around one person, usually a woman under twenty who exhibits signs of emotional distress. Consequently, psychologists now believe that some poltergeist activity may be caused by living beings who are having a psychic reaction to abuse or other traumas.

possession A spirit taking control of another person's body, literally forcing out the residing soul. In earlier history, people with mental disorders and odd physical ailments were considered possessed.

preta In Hindu lore, a tiny spirit that wanders for a year near its old home. Stories of preta indicate that this spirit may belong to a child who died very young. Buddhists believe that rebirth as a preta is due to the karma of greed, and that these beings can live near crossroads and barriers in this world, as well as in their own realm.

psychic Both a noun and an adjective, this term applies to experiences and occurrences that defy conventional ideas about the limits of the human mind and its capacity for extra-sensory awareness. Phenomena in this category include **extra-sensory perception**, auric reading, and **mediumship**. A person with such talents is often called a psychic, seer, or **sensitive**.

querent Someone who poses a question to a diviner.

rapport A connection with the dead, specifically the communion established by a medium through meditation and trance states.

reincarnation The belief that the soul goes into a temporary waiting period after death, and then is reborn into a new body where it can learn lessons necessary to achieve enlightenment. This belief, while most popular in Hindu teachings, also had adherents among the ancient Druids and the Cathars of the Middle Ages. It is also found in some schools of Cabalism and in many Native American traditions.

retzechith chayalalim In Jewish legend, an angelic spirit that bears the gift of life.

St. Elmo's fire St. Elmo, or Erasmus, is the patron saint of sailors. According to legend, he survived a lightning strike. During storms at sea, the appearance of balls of light on top of the ship's mast or a sailor's head is considered a sign of St. Elmo's presence. Although St. Elmo's fire hisses and crackles like normal fire, it does no damage. Instances of St. Elmo's fire have also been noted on land; many are regarded as manifestations of spirits. Scientifically, St. Elmo's fire is thought to be caused by concentrated, charged electrons.

sand altar woman A Hopi Indian spirit who protects women during childbirth, and safeguards game animals from harm.

scrying A form of divination in which a person looks intently at an object, such as a flame or crystal, in order to see images appear in it. These images can be literal or symbolic, and give answers to the questions posed by a querent. Some people feel the images are generated by a spirit.

séance Gatherings guided by **mediums** for the purpose of contacting and communicating with specific disincarnate beings, often the loved ones of those present.

sendings Icelandic term for revenging spirits commanded by a necromancer (see also **necromancy**). The only vulnerable spot on a sending is its white center; if this is speared with iron, the sending is dispelled.

shade Old English word for **ghost**.

smudging Using incense to purify an area of unwanted energies, often with sage.

specter A term for the apparition of a **ghost** or spirit; from the Latin *spectare*, to behold or to look at.

spirit A disembodied intelligence or consciousness, with a definite personality, will, and disposition. From the Latin *spiritus*, meaning breath. This term may also refer to supernatural beings such as fairies and sprites.

spiritualism A religious system with a strong central belief that there is life after death, and that communication with **ghosts** is possible with the aid of a trained **medium**.

supernatural The domain that is beyond nature and ordinary experience, where spirits abide.

swamp gas A natural occurrence often mistaken for a ghostly apparition. Decaying matter in the swamp creates a combustible gas, which may explain sightings like those attributed to the **Will-o'-the-Wisp**.

theomania Possession by a beneficent entity, such as occurs in some channeling sessions. Among some New Age philosophers, this may also be a manifestation of the individual's Higher Self, which creates a persona through which specific ideas or lessons may be imparted.

thought form Energy that takes on partial substance, caused by a frequently recurring thought. For example, someone who focuses on a specific fear may eventually "see" that fear, as a dark, looming cloud.

trance A heightened meditative state in which a person can cross over to, and communicate with, the supernatural world. Shamans, **mediums**, and medicine people from many tribes practice reaching this state for visionary experiences or to prepare for spirit possession.

transmigration The belief that a soul moves from one body to the next through the process of reincarnation. Some cultures believe that a soul can transmigrate into the body of an animal, as well as into a human body.

utburd Scandinavian term for the vengeful ghosts created by sickly infants.

vardger Norwegian version of a **doppelganger** or **fetch**.

vassage The spirit inhabiting a scrying crystal. During scrying sessions, it communicates by forming literal or symbolic visual images.

Will-o'-the-Wisp Also called fox fire, this round flame floats enigmatically in mid-air. Records of this phenomena go back to Roman times. The most common forms of Will-o'-the-Wisp are yellow or blue flames that dance or bob above the ground. In German folklore, the Will-o'-the-Wisp was believed to be a lost or trapped soul, while some Native American traditions regard it as a fire spirit that warns of danger. Some African societies believe that this light comes from a witch who wishes to scare wrongdoers into behaving properly. In Russia, these lights are thought to be the souls of stillborn children. And in other European traditions, these lights are spirits that were too evil to reach heaven, but not so corrupt that they deserved hell. The Latin term for this manifestation is *ignis fatuus*, meaning "fool's fire." This term originated in Rome, where travelers mistook the apparition for the lights of a nearby town. Following this light, the travelers wandered off the road into the swamps.

winti A Guianan spirit that exists without material substance.

wraith A type of **doppelganger** seen at the moment of death, or just prior to it. Wraiths are considered a type of "crisis" ghost—the projected spirit of a person facing mortality, appearing in order to communicate a last message to the living.

Bibliography

Aveni, Anthony. *Behind the Crystal Ball.* NY: Random House, 1996.

Appenzeller, Tim and David Thomson, eds. *Ghosts.* Richmond, VA: Time Life Books, 1984.

Barrett, Sir William F. *Deathbed Visions.* Wellingborough, England: Aquarian Press, 1986.

Blackmore, Sue. *Beyond the Body.* NY: Heinemann, 1982.

Bayless, Raymond. *The Other Side of Death.* New Hyde Park, NY: University Books, 1971.

Brandon, Ruth. *The Spiritualists.* NY: Knopf, 1983.

Cavendish, Richard, ed. *Man, Myth and Magic.* NY: Marshall Cavendish, 1970.

Chaundler, Christine. *Everyman's Book of Superstition.* NY: Philosophical Library, 1970.

Daniels, Pat, ed. *Psychic Voyages.* Richmond, VA: Time Life Books, 1987.

Fiore, Edith. *You Have Been Here Before.* NY: Sphere, 1978.

George, Leonard. *Alternate Realities.* NY: Facts on File, 1995.

Grey, Margot. *Return from Death.* NY: Arkana, 1986.

Guiley, Rosemary Ellen. *Harper's Encyclopedia of Mystical and Paranormal Experience.* NY: Harper Collins, 1991.

Haining, Peter. *Ghosts: The Illustrated History.* Secaucus, NJ: Chartwell Books, 1987.

Horan, Anne, ed. *Psychic Powers.* Richmond, VA: Time Life Books, 1987.

Inglis, Brian. *Natural and Supernatural.* London, England: Hodder &
    Stoughton, 1977.

MacKenzie, Andrew. *Hauntings and Apparitions.* England: Society of
    Psychical Research, 1982.

Moody, Raymond. *Life After Life.* NY: Bantam, 1975.

Myers, Arthur. *Ghostly Register.* NY: Contemporary Books, 1986.

Newall, Venetia. *Encyclopedia of Witchcraft and Magic.* NY: Dial Press,
    1974.

Randles, Jenny, and Peter Hough. *The Afterlife.* NY: Berkley Books, 1993.

Rawcliffe, D.H. *Occult and Supernatural Phenomena.* NY: Dover Books,
    1987.

Telesco, Patricia. *Folkways: Reclaiming the Magic & Wisdom.* St. Paul, MN:
    Llewellyn Publications, 1995.

Underwood, Peter. *The Ghost Hunter's Guide.* Poole, Dorset: Javelin
    Books, 1988.

BOOKS BY THE CROSSING PRESS

A Little Book of Love Magic
By Patricia Telesco

A cornucopia of lore, magic, and imaginative ritual designed to bring excitement and romance to your life. Patricia Telesco tells us how to use magic to manifest our hopes and dreams for romantic relationships, friendships, family relations, and passions for our work.

$9.95 • Paper • ISBN 0-89594-887-7

Casting the Circle: A Women's Book of Ritual
By Diane Stein

A comprehensive guide including 23 full ritual outlines for the waxing, full and waning moons, the eight Sabbats, and rites of passage.

$14.95 • Paper • ISBN 0-89594-411-1

Ariadne's Thread: A Workbook of Goddess Magic
By Shekinah Mountainwater

One of the finest books on women's spirituality available.—Sagewoman
Shekhinah Mountainwater's organized and well-written book encourages women to find their own spiritual path. This is a very good, practical book...recommended.—Library Journal

$16.95 • Paper • ISBN 0-89594-475-8

Channeling for Everyone: A Safe Step-by-Step Guide to Developing Your Intuition and Psychic Awareness
By Tony Neate

This is a clear, concise guide to developing our subtler levels of consciousness. It provides us with safe, step-by-step exercises to prepare for and begin to practice channeling, allowing wider states of consciousness to become part of our everyday lives.

$12.95 • Paper • ISBN 0-89594-922-9

FutureTelling: A Complete Guide to Divination
By Patricia Telesco

This cross-cultural encyclopedia of divination practices gives over 250 entries, from simple signs and omens of traditional folk magic to complex rituals of oracular consultation.

$16.95 • Paper • ISBN 0-89594-872-9

BOOKS BY THE CROSSING PRESS

Pocket Guide to Celtic Spirituality

By Sirona Knight

The Earth-centered philosophy and rituals of ancient Celtic spirituality have special relevance today as we strive to balance our relationship with the planet. This guide offers a comprehensive introduction to the rich religious tradition of the Celts.

$6.95 • Paper • ISBN 0-89594-907-5

Pocket Guide to Fortunetelling

By Scott Cunningham

Pocket Guide to Fortunetelling is a complete guide to determining your past, present, and future. With detailed instructions of over 100 techniques, we find that this ageless art is a powerful ally in reshaping our lives.

$6.95 • Paper • ISBN 0-89594-875-3

Pocket Guide to Numerology

By Alan Oken

Discover the science of numerology. Each chapter begins with a simple formula that helps you discover your personal destiny, understand aspects of your character, or determine the proper time to accomplish a goal

$6.95 • Paper • ISBN 0-89594-826-5

Pocket Guide to Shamanism

By Tom Cowan

Are you intrigued by the mysteries of nature and the realm of the spirit? Have you experienced a magical or mystical occurrence? Perhaps shamanism is calling you. Bringing shamanism into your life can allow you to restore sacred ritual, gain insight, and live with sensitivity and respect for the planet.

$6.95 • Paper • ISBN 0-89594-845-1

Pocket Guide to The Tarot

By Alan Oken

The Tarot has been an ancient source of wisdom and insight into the human heart and mind. The 78 cards of the Tarot deck help you to open a door to higher consciousness, gain insights on the past and present, and discern future directions.

$6.95 • Paper • ISBN 0-89594-822-2

BOOKS BY THE CROSSING PRESS

Prophetic Visions of the Future

By Diane Stein

We all want to know what will happen to the earth and to those who come after us, our children and our grandchildren. Diane, seeking an answer, has gone to women visionaries and seers: women who channel the future and those who bring it to life in their writings: Sally Miller Gearhart, Sheri Tepper, and Marge Piercy.

$16.95 • Paper • ISBN 1-58091-046-7

Psychic Healing with Spirit Guides & Angels

By Diane Stein

A guide to hands-on and psychic healing, this comprehensive book presents a complete program of soul development for self-healing, healing with others, and Earth healing. Advanced skills include healing karma and past lives, soul retrieval, releasing spirit attachments, and understanding and aiding the death process.

$18.95 • Paper • ISBN 0-89594-807-9

Shamanism as a Spiritual Practice for Daily Life

By Tom Cowan

This inspirational book blends elements of shamanism with inherited traditions and contemporary religious commitments. An inspiring spiritual call.—Booklist

$16.95 • Paper • ISBN 0-89594-838-9

Spinning Spells, Weaving Wonders: Modern Magic for Everyday Life

By Patricia Telesco

This essential book of over 300 spells tells how to work with simple, easy-to-find components and focus creative energy to meet daily challenges with awareness, confidence, and humor.

$14.95 • Paper • ISBN 0-89594-803-6

We are the Angels: Healing Your Past, Present, and Future with the Lords of Karma

By Diane Stein

Stein masterfully presents a detailed understanding of karma and the process of healing karmic patterns. She introduces the Lords of Karma, the supreme karmic record keepers able to grant requests for changed or released karma to those who ask for it.

$16.95 • Paper • ISBN 0-89594-878-8

BOOKS BY THE CROSSING PRESS

Wind and Water: Your Personal Feng Shui Journey

By Carol J. Hyder

This book presents Feng Shui as simple suggestions that can be done on a daily basis-each page will provide information and a corresponding activity. Instead of reading about Feng Shui, this book will provide an immediate experience of Feng Shui.

$19.95 • Paper • ISBN 1-58091-050-5

Wisdom of the Elements: The Sacred Wheel of Earth, Air, Fire and Water

By Margie McArthur

Drawing on her knowledge of neo-pagan tradition, as well as Traditional Chinese Medicine, energy work with the chakras, and Native American wisdom, McArthur gives us keys to the intricate correspondences between the Elements, the planet and our psychic landscape.

$16.95 • Paper • ISBN 0-89594-936-9

A Wisewoman's Guide to Spells, Rituals and Goddess Lore

By Elizabeth Brooke

A remarkable compendium of magical lore, psychic skills and women's mysteries.

$12.95 • Paper • ISBN 0-89594-779-X

Wishing Well: Empowering Your Hopes and Dreams

By Patricia Telesco

Blending folklore, magic, and creative visualization, author Patricia Telesco explains how reclaiming the practice of Wishcraft can create our reality exactly as we wish it to be.

$14.95 • Paper • ISBN 0-89594-870-2

To receive a current catalog from The Crossing Press
please call toll-free, 800-777-1048.
Visit our Web site: **www.crossingpress.com**